Annabel Beeforth

Style Me Vintage

An inspirational guide to styling
the perfect vintage wedding

weddings

CHICAGO
REVIEW
PRESS

Contents

INTRODUCTION

The feelings a woman experiences upon finding *the* wedding dress are a mix of excitement, exhilaration, wonderment, and awe. If only you could bottle the feeling, you'd be a sure-fire millionaire. There is something about the experience of wearing a wedding dress that has always thrilled and intoxicated women, but never more so than in the past century, when bridal fashion became big business. Dresses changed from being furbelowed, formal, corseted, and restrictive to the far more relaxed, fluid, comfortable, and flattering silhouette we see today. Given that a wedding dress is probably the most expensive item of clothing most women will ever buy, it holds great emotional significance. It will steal the limelight on the wedding day and be talked about for years after. Many dresses are so esteemed – they become much-loved heirlooms – pass-me-downs for the younger generation to keep safe and maybe wear again.

The popularity of original vintage or vintage-inspired bridal fashion has soared in recent years. As a consequence, the original vintage wedding gown has become a valuable and sought-after commodity, and many businesses have been set up to specialize in the supply of original vintage wedding dresses or modern replicas. Even designer brands are hopping on board, creating pieces in their latest collections that pay homage to the popular styles of the past.

Subconsciously I always knew I was a lover of vintage style, but it didn't become evident to me until 2007, when I set off on a fifteen-month journey to plan my own nuptials. During my research, I found myself drawn time and time again to glamorous, floor-sweeping, red carpet-inspired gowns reminiscent of the deco fashions of the 1930s that look just as gorgeous today as they did back then. In the end, I opted for a Jenny Packham design that wouldn't have looked out of place on Marlene Dietrich or Greta Garbo, with Art Deco detailing and panel beading around the bust and what seemed like miles of silk charmeuse draping to the floor behind me and trailing into the most elegant of trains. I was smitten. I felt like a million dollars. It was then that I discovered my passion for vintage and vintage-inspired bridal wear and it has been a true love of mine ever since.

Through *Style Me Vintage: Weddings,* I aim to bring my adoration of vintage bridal fashion and my passion for weddings together in one useful, inspirational resource. I am a firm advocate of working with a professional event stylist on the style aspects of your wedding day, but this book will provide some great starting points and ideas for how you can style your own vintage-inspired wedding.

The book provides a potted history lesson of bridal fashion, decade-by-decade, from the Edwardian era to the 1970s. Original vintage wedding photography and historical facts and references will help you understand the bridal styles of the time, as well as contextualize these fashions against their cultural and social backdrop. Styled photographs will suggest how you can replicate the looks of that particular era, focusing on fashion, beauty, detail and décor. The images have been styled using a mix of original and replica vintage wedding elements and have been designed to inspire and encourage you to try different things, to mix and match until you find your own personal vintage style. Each chapter ends with a look at how real brides have incorporated a vintage-inspired look into their own wedding day. Towards the back of the book, you will find detailed lists of recommended suppliers and online resources.

Style Me Vintage: Weddings has by no means been produced for those who consider themselves "purist" in vintage terms. Rather, it has been created to inspire any bride interested in vintage wedding style, no matter on what scale. Whether you choose to simply dip your toes into the rich pool of vintage fashion or go diving in head-first, the inspiration and advice contained in this book will help make your vintage wedding experience fun, satisfying, and rewarding.

I do hope that when you finish reading this book, you will feel inspired, and just a little bit more in love with vintage wedding style.

WHAT IS A VINTAGE WEDDING?

There is something ineffably fascinating about using something old to celebrate something new. Until fairly recently, the tradition of incorporating "something old" into your wedding might have included borrowing a piece of jewelry from a close friend or family member. Nowadays, couples have realized that they can personalize their entire wedding day by styling it according to the fashions and aesthetics of an era that they admire.

The term "vintage wedding" tends to provoke a love/hate response; purists reject the loose application of the term in regard to weddings with a subtle reference towards the past, and some wedding industry professionals have turned their back on the use of the term altogether – possibly fearful that the perceived trend will pass or become unpopular, and weary of how the description has proliferated the wedding blog community. Like it or not, there is no denying the beauty and appeal of a vintage wedding dress and all that exquisite craftsmanship and attention to detail, or of the elegant accessories rediscovered after years tucked away in storage boxes, or of the heirloom veil that your grandma wore at her own wedding.

The way I see it, fashions and styles of the past are timeless, beautiful pieces of history that should be accessible to all who admire them today, including brides. "Vintage wedding" is simply a descriptive term applied to evoke the style and aesthetic chosen by a modern bride or couple, which reflects a major element of their wedding day. And, for me, an original vintage dress or replica vintage dress is the first qualifier of a vintage wedding.

Regardless, whether you opt for a full-on, authentic vintage affair, or a more vintage-inspired wedding with just a few light references to a bygone era, what really matters is that your day reflects your personal tastes and preferences. Craft your wedding by cherry-picking the details you love the most. There are no hard and fast rules when it comes to vintage wedding style and this book will encourage you to be as creative or varied in your style as you like. Explore and discover different eras—mix and match various looks if you so wish. It's entirely up to you.

WHY WEAR VINTAGE?

Grab yourself a telephone directory or check any online search engine and you'll soon be able to locate the details of a seamstress, designer, or tailor who should be able to produce a replica vintage wedding dress at your request. Rip out the pages of a magazine and take these "tear sheets" along to early meetings with your seamstress or designer and he or she will be able to draw up ideas and create a "toile" (an initial mockup of a design, often created in cheap fabric such as calico, in order to perfect a bespoke cut and fit before the final design is produced in the chosen fabrics). This bespoke option is a popular choice amongst brides who are inspired by vintage wedding fashions but may be cautious about investing in an original vintage design.

But original vintage is not something to be afraid of. Although it is a known fact that most vintage wedding gowns tend to be small in fit (particularly around the waist), can carry imperfections or be damaged, this shouldn't discourage you from exploring the past to find something beautiful and unique to wear on your wedding day.

"Fashions fade, style is eternal ..." Yves Saint Laurent

Deciding to wear an authentic vintage wedding dress has several key benefits:

* **One of a kind** Every vintage wedding dress available today is a one-off—a completely unique piece of history that you can guarantee will not be seen on any other bride, no matter how many wedding magazines or wedding blogs you browse through. The vintage wedding dress wardrobe offers rich pickings too, with over 100 years of styles available.

* **Current fashions and trends aren't important** Researching what vintage looks you love the most will help you to discover more about your own personal style and what works best with your body shape.

* **Fine craftsmanship** Most vintage wedding dresses were produced prior to mass commercial manufacturing and thus boast beautiful craftsmanship and attention to detail.

* **Value for money** Almost all original vintage wedding dresses are less expensive than modern-day replicas or designer wedding dresses (although some designer vintage bridal gowns, whose provenance can be traced, will be much more expensive and available only via auction or specialists with a niche in designer vintage).

* **A style to suit every body shape** Certain era looks tend to favor particular body types and each chapter ahead will touch on this in more detail. For example the more loose, dropped-waist looks of the 1920s tend to better suit a more slender frame and smaller bust; the fluid bias-cut styles of the 1930s suit tall slender figures, but also look amazing on curves; and the fuller-skirted, layered petticoat look that became popular in the 1950s will flatter the fuller figure.

* **Recycling Fashion** Those with environmentally-friendly preferences can feel satisfied knowing that a vintage wedding dress is effectively being "recycled" and given a new lease of life.

* **Ethical** On the whole, choosing to wear vintage presents a better choice ethically: with the exception of bespoke dressmaking, most (though by no means all) contemporary wedding dress manufacture takes place overseas, utilizing low-cost commercial production services. This raises an ethical question mark when a wedding dress is then sold for many times more than the amount that it cost to manufacture because it holds a designer name tag—or, more often than not, simply because it is a wedding dress.

BUYING AN ORIGINAL VINTAGE WEDDING DRESS

Vintage wedding dresses are more accessible now than ever before: check your local vintage clothing stores or resale shops; visit a specialist boutique; view online auctions, such as eBay; browse through an independent online store or the fabulous Etsy.com marketplace; or visit a vintage wedding fair and you will soon find yourself immersed in a world of original vintage bridal fashion. Whichever way you prefer to approach your vintage wedding dress shopping experience, there are a few things you need to know before you do.

✳ **Know your measurements** This especially applies when shopping online or at a vintage wedding fair (a specialist boutique owner will take your measurements for you). You need to be aware of your neck, bust, waist, hip, and thigh measurements–even your cuff measurements for dresses with long sleeves. A great online measuring guide is located at www.wikihow.com/Take-Clothing-Measurements.

✳ **If possible, try before you buy** It is always a good idea to take shoes similar in heel height to the ones you will be wearing on your wedding day to any fitting–and remember to take any shapewear you may wish to help further define your silhouette. If shopping online, ask for dress measurements (waist, chest, neck, cuff, and dress length) and check to see if the seller has a returns policy. Don't let this dissuade you from purchasing online or from overseas–buying direct is often cheaper.

✳ **Check the condition of the dress for damage and deterioration** Since most vintage wedding dresses have been worn just once, many of them are in near-perfect condition, with gentle wear and tear evident from the passing of time. Don't be put off by these imperfections–they can add to the overall charm and unique character of the dress. Some gowns may carry significant imperfections that you will want to consider more carefully before making any purchase. Don't fret–use the pointers below to assist:

General deterioration Before the introduction of man-made fibers in the 30s and 40s, dresses were made using natural fibers, which also have a natural life span. Silk will begin to deteriorate after around 50 years. This means that dresses pre-dating the mid-1930s may not be as well preserved as dresses created after this time. They are also more likely to be more expensive, given their scarcity.

Fastenings Do they work? Are buttons missing? Are zippers still functional or will they need replacing?

Stains and marks Never assume a stain can be removed. Check the armpit area for permanent sweat damage (not a good look on your wedding day!). Is the dress marked in any way? Will the marks be very obvious or can they be concealed? Can the seller recommend a specialist cleaning company? NEVER send a vintage wedding dress to the dry cleaners; ALWAYS entrust an original vintage gown with a specialist experienced in restoring vintage dresses to their former glory.

Tears, rips, and holes Can these be mended over or concealed? A pretty cover-up may help to disguise any irreparable damage or minor imperfections. Consider an original vintage or faux fur shrug or shawl, or invest in an authentic or replica beaded cape.

✳ **Sizing** Body shapes have altered considerably over the past century (largely because we are better fed these days and not having to survive on war rations!). It was also quite normal for brides in the past to wear corsetry that drew in their waists to much smaller proportions than we are used to today. Thus, vintage wedding dresses are often quite small in fit.

To be safe, I recommend you assume that any size referenced in labeling will fit today's bride who measures one size, possibly even two sizes, smaller. A garment marked UK 12/US 10/EU 40 is likely to fit a modern day UK 10/US 8/EU 38, or even the next size down. Remember also that dresses that pre-date the mid-century are unlikely to carry a size label at all—these dresses were often homemade or produced by a tailor as a one-off design.

The majority of vintage wedding dresses available today will fit the modern day sizes UK 8-14/US 6-12/EU 36-42, with smaller sizes being more widely available. But don't despair! Dresses in larger sizes are out there; they are just a little more difficult to come by.

✳ **Fit and Alterations** Never be put off by a vintage dress that doesn't fit perfectly when you first try it on—even if you can't close it up at all. It may be possible to make alterations, even if this involves some major reconstruction. A good tailor or seamstress will be able to come up with creative solutions to dresses that are too small to fit. Alterations to the length, neckline, and the removal/addition of sleeves may help to transform your amazing vintage find into your perfect wedding dress.

NEVER try to squeeze yourself into something that is simply far too small. You want to feel and look fabulous on your wedding day. Attempting the "big squeeze" is always a mistake and stretching delicate vintage fabrics could destroy the dress beyond repair.

Remember to ask how much alterations are likely to cost before committing to them, to avoid any unwelcome surprises when the bill needs to be paid. And if original vintage doesn't feel right to you, a bespoke alternative that authentically replicates your favorite vintage style or that incorporates various vintage styles in one look is the ideal solution.

Edwardian Era
(the early 1900s)

It was important to me to feature a small chapter on the Edwardian era; it's a fascinating period of wedding history that is often overlooked in bridal fashion, although the hit period drama TV series *Downton Abbey* has done much to draw attention to the fabulous fashions of these times.

It is still possible to find exquisite, original Edwardian wedding gowns that are in good enough condition to wear today. I would strongly recommend you consult a specialist vintage wedding dress supplier, although it is possible to obtain bargains via sites like Etsy and eBay. Original Edwardian wedding gowns were constructed before the introduction of man-made fibers and, of course, with most now more than one hundred years old, they are more fragile than other vintage wedding dresses, and more scarce. You may prefer to have a replica gown made. Do your research, gather images online, select your favorite elements from each dress (the neckline, the embroidered detail, the sleeve, etc.) and take them to a dressmaker to talk through your ideas.

Dress style best suited to:
those who enjoy a more demure, elegantly modest look.

Key bridal looks of the period:
- Hourglass silhouette
- An all-concealed look; high neckline, three-quarter to full-length "leg o' mutton" sleeves
- High waistline—the "empire line"
- Cummerbunds and sashes—popular in the mid-late Edwardian period
- Tiered lace and light, floaty chiffon
- Hair done up high and large decorated hats/headpieces with long veils
- Long gloves
- Pearl or beaded bridal collars
- Headpieces made from wax orange blossom flowers
- Gold and pastel color schemes
- Corsets

FASHION

The Edwardian period was an age of industrialization and innovation, and a time when women's roles in society were changing radically in response to historical turning points such as World War I and the suffragette movement. Bridal fashions were influenced heavily by the wedding of Queen Victoria in the previous century, who chose to marry her cousin Albert of Saxe-Coburg in a white wedding dress, with orange blossom (symbolizing purity) and myrtle (symbolizing love and domestic happiness) in her hair. Common belief would have it that, prior to this, brides only wore dresses in their favorite color, but that's not entirely true; many brides could not afford to buy a dress just for their wedding day and so wore their best (usually colored) dresses instead. White was worn prior to this, often signifying family wealth, but became the color of choice for most brides after Queen Victoria wore it for her wedding in 1840. The wedding was widely publicized and inspired new generations of brides to copy her style.

The style of the Edwardian wedding dress was purposefully all-concealing. It was considered bad form to expose any flesh, even the neck and arms, so full-length sleeves were common, or three-quarter-length sleeves worn with long gloves. The neckline was often concealed entirely by a "wedding collar"–a wide band of pearls, or jeweled piece of fabric–and a modesty panel of fabric would conceal the

Top and above: Typical Edwardian bridal fashion included a wide-brimmed hat. It was common for a single wedding photograph to be taken during this time, involving the bride seated next to the groom.

area between the bustline and the neck. Dresses featured an abundance of embroidered lace, delicate silk, chiffons, and embellishment. Long veils, which were thought to keep evil at bay, would sit atop hair that had been styled high on top of the head. The silhouette during the earlier part of the era was defined by corsetry. The "S-shape" corset was designed to thrust forward a woman's best assets, and pull her tummy area inward, creating an almost faux-bustle look from behind—the voluptuous cleavage shape created by the corsetry would be on show in the evening, never in the day.

Left: This photo was taken by the well-known Belgian photographer Ferdinand Buyle at a wedding in Brussels, 1912.

Right: A wedding portrait of Eleanor Clay Ford, the bride of Henry Ford's son Edsel, 1916.

The modest aesthetic became more relaxed as the 1920s approached. Hemlines rose throughout the period, and by the end of World War I the "new woman" had arrived, ready to take on the excitement and the fabulously fun flapper-girl style of the Roaring Twenties.

REAL BRIDE

TAMSIN & ALEX'S WEDDING
SEPTEMBER 18, 2010

Dress Original vintage Edwardian wedding dress.

Accessories Vintage 1920s veil and hair accessory; the original 1950s bracelet was my grandma's; my 1930s engagement ring was Alex's grandma's.

Shoes Department store.

What inspired you to wear a beautiful original Edwardian wedding dress? It just fitted what I was looking for—it ticked every box. I loved the detail of the tactile fabric—every other lace dress I tried felt so sterile and manufactured in comparison. I also liked the conservative silhouette. I knew I wanted sleeves, as a strapless dress wouldn't have felt right at the altar. Although I don't wear a lot of vintage clothes, I have always loved the historic reference of a beautiful piece of clothing or jewelry. I am also fascinated by the way vintage or antique items can suddenly become timeless.

What do you love most about the dress? The fabric—it felt both striking and romantic.

Wedding décor and details The wedding wasn't supposed to be vintage style per se, but we did enjoy making contextual references to the seaside town where we married. We sent handwritten vintage Torquay postcards as invitations and I made the menus out of the same imagery. The wedding was made up of all our favorite things and I enjoyed mixing the old with the new (for example the bridesmaids wore short shift dresses). It was a complete coincidence, but my Mum also wore an Edwardian dress and was married in the same church!

Advice for other brides who love Edwardian style? For me, it wasn't an easy look to pull together—especially knowing what shoes to wear with this style! Although feeling like I didn't have any precedents to follow for the dress, as well as the whole wedding, was absorbing and exciting. I think it's all about feeling comfortable and confident.

REAL BRIDE

JANE AND DYLAN'S WEDDING
AUGUST 20, 2011

Dress I found the dress online—it's an original Edwardian wedding dress. As soon as I saw the photos, I fell in love with it and couldn't let it go to someone else! My mother, who is an incredible seamstress, agreed it was worth restoring for me. She altered the dress to fit me, adding beautiful details along the way, such as mother of pearl fastenings. The original slip had disintegrated over time, so she made a new one. Thankfully, apart from some minor marks, the lace was in incredible condition considering the dress dates from around 1910.

Accessories I wore a faux-pearl necklace given to me by Dylan's mom, which had belonged to her grandmother. They're such a beautiful color, and helped us to choose the dusty pink slip. It was a privilege to wear them, and I continue to treasure them. As a hair accessory, I restored tiny silk pink flowers that I found in a thrift shop and attached them to hairgrips.

Shoes Secondhand from eBay. They were by Diane Hassall and called "Liliana."

What inspired you to wear a beautiful Edwardian wedding dress? I didn't originally set out to find an Edwardian dress, but knew that I wanted vintage. I had grown up watching Fred Astaire and Ginger Rogers films, and I love the 30s for its dresses. I found quite a few original dresses at vintage fairs from that era that were too small so, in the end, I widened the search to anything vintage that looked interesting. As it turned out, the dress I ended up with was more beautiful than anything else I had come across, and suited my shape far better than a 30s dress! I loved that it was over a hundred years old and was in such good condition. To think of all the women that had worn and loved it as much as I did on my wedding day was just perfect.

What do you love most about the dress? The hand embroidery on the lace is very beautiful and intricate and must have taken a long time to make. I love to think about the history behind the dress. Who made it and who wore it first?

Wedding décor and details I collected vintage tablecloths to place over straw bales, which I plan to make into a quilt as a keepsake of the day.

The 1920s

The 1920s heralded a time of optimism following the end of World War I. The decade saw in huge social change: women gained the vote for the first time in the United States and the United Kingdom, and Prohibition took hold in America. Socialites and aristocrats went out and had a riot. They donned elaborate fancy dress, got drunk, smoked, and partook in many a reckless activity. This young and carefree collective were labeled "The Bright Young Things" by the press and, while their lifestyles were extravagant, they came to represent the zeitgeist. Free-spirited and fun-loving, these hedonistic, raucous times became known as the Roaring Twenties. These societal changes were reflected in fashion and, ultimately, bridal fashions of the time.

The arts and culture scene flourished during the 1920s. Art Deco and Surrealism were established and the Jazz Age had arrived. Early cinema proved hugely influential too. Silent black and white movies featured the likes of Louise Brooks, Josephine Baker, and Greta Garbo, but it was Clara Bow who captured the imagination of the adoring public. Bow oozed on-screen sex appeal and her cinematic performances liberated a whole generation of young women, including brides. She was the true It girl of the time—a fabulously flirtatious flapper girl, chopping up her dresses on screen with scissors to make them sexier and more appealing to the catch she had her eye on.

World War I had resulted in the "lost generation": hundreds of young men had lost their lives in battle. Because of this, the ratio of potential male suitors to suitable brides was low and so not all women could assume they would end up marrying at all. Nevertheless, weddings in the 20s were, in keeping with the party atmosphere of the times, much more informal, celebratory events. Elopements became popular in the 1920s too, as did wedding and engagement rings that matched—platinum and white gold being the choice of most.

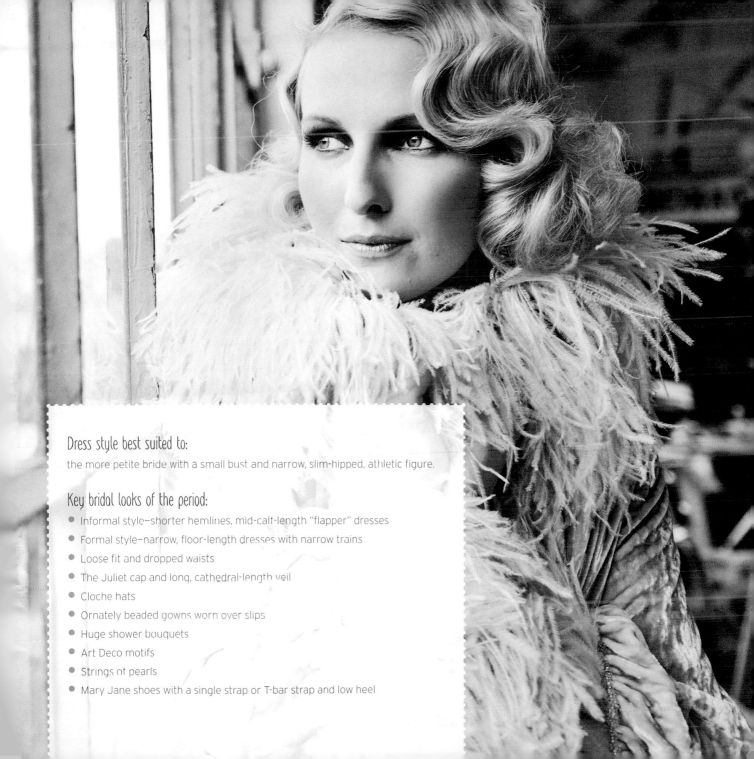

Dress style best suited to:

the more petite bride with a small bust and narrow, slim-hipped, athletic figure.

Key bridal looks of the period:

- Informal style—shorter hemlines, mid-calf-length "flapper" dresses
- Formal style—narrow, floor-length dresses with narrow trains
- Loose fit and dropped waists
- The Juliet cap and long, cathedral-length veil
- Cloche hats
- Ornately beaded gowns worn over slips
- Huge shower bouquets
- Art Deco motifs
- Strings of pearls
- Mary Jane shoes with a single strap or T-bar strap and low heel

VINTAGE INSPIRATION

Left: A bridal model wearing a brocade wedding dress in 1921, with lace bertha and large tulle veil held in place by a strand of pearls.

Above: A bride and groom in Rome, Italy, 1929.

Above: Frank Raw and Ethel Beeforth married April 24, 1920, in North Yorkshire, England.

Right: Cover of *The Tatler*, 1927, featuring the wedding of WWI flying ace Captain Alec Cunningham-Reid to Hon. Ruth Mary Clarisse Ashley. They were described as "England's wealthiest girl and handsomest man."

CAPTAIN AND MRS. A. S. CUNNINGHAM REID

Above: Art Deco fashion sketch of a bridal gown made of soft satin or charmeuse and a veil of old lace, 1921.

FASHION

Not happy with the corseted, restricted styles of the Edwardian period, Madame Coco Chanel was busy making history by redefining the female silhouette. She cast away the corset and designed clothes that focused less on the feminine form, and more on function. Chanel wanted women to feel comfortable and to allow them more freedom to move –her designs echoed the social changes of the time. She is credited with introducing the loose "sack" style and dropped-waist look that is now associated with the 1920s.

Flapper girls took to this new fashion like a cat mopping up cream. The nightclubs were soon full of performers and revellers, resplendent in beaded and tasseled frocks–strings of pearls and elaborate headpieces completing their look. The "flapper" was the good-time girl who dared to break all the rules and party like she didn't care. Eventually, this new look filtered through to bridalwear. A sleeveless flapper-style dress falling at calf length, worn over a simple slip was the choice of many. This fuss-free dress shape provided the perfect opportunity for embellishment, such as exquisite and ornate beading and Art Deco-inspired decorative features.

It is possible to source an original 20s wedding dress that can be worn today, but expect original dresses in good condition to be pretty scarce and, as a result, more expensive. As most dresses of the time were made from pure silk, they are likely to carry some damage due to natural deterioration over time.

Left: The "Goodbye to Berlin" opera coat (from the Beautiful and the Damned collection by Joanne Fleming), named for the Christopher Isherwood novellas that introduced the flapper character Sally Bowles to the world.

Right: A selection of replica 1920s dresses, from left to right: "Sienna" by Caroline Atelier for Luella's Boudoir, silk and satin with glass beading; a short beaded flapper-style dress from the State of Grace; "Rebecca" and "Primrose" by Vicky Rowe for Luella's Boudoir, drawing upon style influences from the 20s and 30s, each dress has been exquisitely designed and features hand-finished embroidery and beading.

Above and right: The "Maimuna" dress by Charlotte Casadéjus is entirely covered in antique French and English lace dating from 1880 to 1920.

Opposite: A delicately hand-beaded cloche hat bridal headpiece by designer Edwina Ibbotson.

Silk tends to "shatter" after about 50 years, but it may be possible for damaged features to be repaired or replaced by a speciality alterations service. Speciality vintage wedding dress suppliers will be the best to advise you, but do your research online too.

If you adore the styles of the 1920s but are concerned about finding a suitable original dress, consider a bespoke replica. There are a number of contemporary bridalwear designers that have used the 1920s as inspiration for their designs: Lindsay Fleming's "All That Jazz" collection (www.lindsayfleming.com) was inspired by the Roaring Twenties and comprises eight dresses and a coat, each of which have been carefully and exquisitely fashioned on the styles of the time. My favorite dress from this collection is "Clara," named after the iconic silent movie star Clara Bow. Its skirt is made from 20 meters of pure silk tulle and adorned with feathers, which float elegantly as you

walk—true 20s glamour. Other designers who have looked to the 20s for design inspiration include Jenny Packham (www.jennypackham.com), the Vintage Wedding Dress Company (www.thevintageweddingdresscompany.com), Sue Wong (www.suewong.com), Zoe Lem (www.zoelem.co.uk), and Sally Lacock (www.sallylacock.com), to name a few.

Fully-beaded dresses can be produced as one-off bespoke designs, but expect to pay a premium. Modern-day replica beaded flapper dresses, manufactured in larger quantities by companies like Leluxe (www.leluxeclothing.com), are a good option and represent truly excellent value.

The flapper-style wedding dress wasn't the only style worn during this period. A more formal gown would have been a narrow floor-length dress that also featured a narrow train. This style of 20s dress is probably better suited to those who don't want to wear a shorter gown on their wedding day.

Veils were typically very long, mostly cathedral length, and featured exquisite lace trim. The Juliet cap veil is one of my favorite styles of the 1920s. This particular style of veil, that rests over the forehead, was originally fashioned in the sixteenth century. The name stems from Shakespeare's play *Romeo and Juliet* (original drawings of Juliet depicted her wearing a cap that fit neatly to the top of her head). Both Kate Moss and Lily Allen chose to wear a Juliet cap veil for their weddings in 2011, and this has sparked a huge resurgence in the popularity of this particular design. Cloche hat-style headpieces with veils attached were also fashionable.

For lovely modern-day interpretations of the cloche hat and Juliet cap veil, check the Accessories listings at the back of this book for inspiration, but look out for Twigs and Honey, an Etsy store that ships worldwide (www.twigsandhoney.com) and LoveBySusie (www.lovebysusie.co.uk).

Instead of wearing a headpiece over the top of your head, tilt it forward to rest across your forehead. The decorated part of the headpiece will come even more into focus and create a bigger wow-factor.

Bridal shoes were the typical Mary Jane style—low-heeled, round-toe designs with either a single bar or T-bar fastening, which provided comfort during all that dancing! Modern shoes in this style are adorned with sparkly embellishment in the shape of Art Deco motifs, or pretty shoe clips featuring feathers. Two of the best shoe designers who take inspiration from the 20s are Rachel Simpson (www.rachelsimpsonshoes.co.uk) and Emmy Scarterfield (www.emmyshoes.co.uk). All Emmy shoes are bespoke designs, so you can influence the heel height, embellishment, and general shape of the shoe.

Beaded handbags and purses made for elegant accessories and were very popular during the 1920s; many modern-day vintage-inspired accessory designers collect pieces like these to sell to their customers. Always ask if they have anything in stock, or refer to a specialized collector such as www. passionateaboutvintage.co.uk. Of course, if you would rather, many department stores offer brilliant replica Art Deco beaded purses. Either way, something in which to keep your lipstick and a pretty monogrammed vintage handkerchief to capture those wedding day tears will prove very useful on your big day!

Finish off your 20s look with strings of pearls, peacock feather accessories, feather buttonholes, and marabou feather fans. Britten Bags design some beautiful feather fan accessories that make pretty gifts for your bridesmaids, or wonderful keepsakes and wedding favors for your female guests.

Opposite: The Ilsadora dress by Sally Lacock.

Top: Jazz Age sparkle and feather vintage bridal cap from the Millésime 2012 Collection by Victoria Millésime.

Above: Antique circlet of flowers, handcrafted petal by petal with clay, by Lila

Left: 1920s-inspired Eva shoes, featuring crystal and pearl encrusted T-bars by Emmy.

29

THE 1920S BRIDE

Many people associate the 1920s with dropped-waist, beaded flapper frocks, but I was keen to explore a less clichéd and more accessible look. Here, Claire wears the "Isadora" dress by Sally Lacock. This asymmetric draped silk chiffon dress with a lace sash and handmade silk flowers is reminiscent of the classical, less structured style adopted by bohemians at the end of the Edwardian era and during the early 1920s. The top chiffon layer drapes gracefully from the hip to form an integral flower; the chiffon is caught up at one side of the hem, revealing a silk charmeuse underlayer. A long train gently flows from the back neckline and can be elegantly draped over the arm (see page 28).

Here a loose fitting and flattering dress design by Katya Katya Shehurina features a dropped waist that was very typical of bridal fashion in the 1920s. The look is set off with original early twentieth century dress ornaments that have been restored and reworked into a flapper-style headpiece by Cherished Vintage. Claire also wears a Juliet cap-style veil by Madeline Bride. This 20s-inspired look is completed with a more dramatic make-up style that remains true to the era, with deep red lips and plum coloured rouge.

BEAUTY

The focus was on looking young and beautiful in the 1920s, but, despite this, makeup was worn quite heavily. A makeup revolution really took off during this era, led by the flapper girls. The young girls were showing the older generations of women how they wanted to do it. Young girls were also being influenced by brands who targeted them through cinema advertisements. It was *the* thing to have a small collection of cosmetics in your handbag, and be at the ready for a touch-up at any time.

Makeup in the 1920s tended to focus on a dramatic look. Eyebrows were fashioned into long thin arches and cupid's bow lips were defined with deep red, brown, and plum colored rouge. Kohl eye liner was used to emphasize the eyes. If dark red lipstick isn't your thing, try a paler, more creamy lip color. This looks fabulous with a smouldering smoky eye—a look made very fashionable once again by the flapper girls of the decade.

If you're applying your own wedding makeup, there are several DIY video make-up tutorials online, including the basics of foundation application, but also how to apply the perfect red lip and smoky eye (see www.lovemydress.net/blog/beauty-tutorials). Twenties eyes were sultry and alluring, so experiment with eye shadow shades including charcoal gray, green, and turquoise—these were all popular colors.

For an authentic manicure, have your nails painted only in the nail center, so the half moon and tip of the nail is left bare, or, for a modern-day twist, paint the half moon a different color. Try experimenting with silvers, golds, creams, and reds.

As the hemlines became shorter in the 1920s, so did hairstyles! Most women started to fashion themselves after the flapper girls, many sporting Louise Brooks-style fringed bobs. This style looks fabulous on the modern-day bride, especially when worn with a dramatic 20s-style headpiece across the forehead.

My personal favorite hairstyle that emerged in the 1920s is the finger wave. I adore the elegance of this hairstyle. Creating a beautiful finger wave is a very special skill and not all hairdressers can pull it off with perfection, so, if you wish to re-create this look, make sure you arrange a hair trial before your wedding day.

DÉCOR AND DETAILS

Turn to cultural references to help inspire the style of your wedding day. There is nothing more fascinating than immersing yourself in a bygone era and imagining what it must have been like for the people of the time. Consider what level of vintage look you are trying to achieve: do you want to recreate a full 1920s party scene at your reception, with your guests dressing up for the occasion too, or would you rather keep things simpler, with subtle nods to the era in the décor?

If you are seeking a light-touch reference to this era, you can retain a sense of the times by referencing Art Deco motifs in your stationery and cake design. Utilize authentic period fonts in your stationery. Some stationery companies can even recreate the style of a tabloid newspaper for you, using fonts and images that would have been popular at the time. Consider having some 20s-style signage created by a stationery designer; take a look at Lucy Ledger's Silent Film collection, reminiscent of the text stills that appeared in the silent movies (www.lucyledger.com).

Consider hosting a speakeasy-style evening reception—this will guarantee that your guests experience a fun, let-your-hair-down kind of atmosphere. Include a secret password in your wedding invites to add some tongue-in-cheek humor. Create cocktails and name them after the silver-screen stars of the era. Hire a vintage china tea service and have waitresses dressed in flapper frocks and headbands serve guests martinis and gin in teacups. Gambling was rife in the 20s, so consider having a poker table and putting out packs of cards for your guests.

HERE ARE SOME CULTURAL REFERENCES TO INSPIRE YOU:

- Art Deco
- Black and white, or gold
- Speakeasy bars
- Silent movies
- Jazz music: the Charleston and the Lindy Hop
- Essential reading: F. Scott Fitzgerald's *The Great Gatsby* and *The Beautiful and Damned*
- Feathers and long strings of pearls
- Headbands and cloche hats
- The gangster scene—Al Capone
- Flapper girls
- The Cotton Club and Ragtime Band
- For men: fedoras, English driving caps, zoot suits, Wing-tip shoes
- Model-T Fords
- Victrolas

Right: Black and gold are synonymous with the strong, rich feel of Art Deco. This 1920s-inspired cake by Olofson Design uses a twenty-four-carat gold geometric pattern on one side of the square tiers to create a style that is both luxe and modern.

If you're a fan, the hit TV series *Boardwalk Empire* is full of inspiration for imitating a stylish speakeasy. Also look to the film *Chicago*, featuring Catherine Zeta-Jones, for inspiration.

For entertainment, a speciality 1920s band would soon have your guests up on their feet and attempting their best performance of the Lindy Hop. Or you might want to consider hiring a cabaret to perform renditions of old jazz songs that would have been popular in 20s nightclubs. Gig Masters (www.gigmasters.com) is a helpful resource for finding local bands such as these.

You can also rent furniture and props that suit this period, such as Art Deco-style backdrops and mirrored drinks bars, but talk to your older relations too—do they have any vintage paraphernalia from the era that would make beautiful props at your wedding? A fabulous scene to set for your gift and cards table would be to find an old Victrola (garage sale? your grandparents' attic?) and fill it with blooms so that it is bursting with color.

For florals, consider replicating one of the huge shower bouquets that featured long trailing foliage. Bouquets of the time were large and elaborate, and tended to be white in color, incorporating blooms like orchids and lilies, orange blossom, gardenias, jasmine and myrtle. A modern-day interpretation could be bursting with all kinds of hues, however. Also consider decorating your bouquet with ostrich feathers and trailing pearls and ribbons. A beautiful alternative for brides who don't want to carry a large bouquet around could be the wrist corsage. These delicate corsages also make a beautiful floral accessory for your bridesmaids too.

Of course, if you truly do want to get into the spirit of things, then encourage your guests to adhere to a dress code, or put out feather boas, long pearl necklaces (you can buy them for next to nothing at your local mall), and gangster hats for them to dress up in.

Ideas for women: Flapper dresses, feather boas, beaded or feathered headbands, long pearl string necklaces, and ostrich feather fans.
Ideas for men: Spats, fedoras, gangster hats, and zoot suits.

The name of the game in the 20s was to be a little wild, so let your hair down and have fun!

Opposite: Original *Vogue* magazine from October 1925. I purchased this magazine from eBay in 2011. It still had its original subscription card inside, which back then cost just $5 a year.

Right: A selection of 1920s Art Deco-inspired wedding stationery by Dottie Creations that coordinates with the cake design on page 37 and features typical 1920s fonts.

39

REAL BRIDE

VICKY & ADAM'S WEDDING
AUGUST 15, 2009

Dress Replica 1920s beaded flapper dress from Sassy and Boo, a vintage shop in Brighton, England.

Accessories The headpiece was made fom an antique 1920s dress clip and I wore a mixture of modern costume and antique pearls.

What inspired you to wear a beautiful 1920s flapper-style dress? I'd been obsessed with 1920s actresses Louise Brooks and Clara Bow for some time. During the run up to the wedding I was immersing myself in literature (*The Great Gatsby*, of course)—books about the fashions of the 1920s, and how beautiful cloche hats were made (I run a business making my own: http://clarabows.co.uk.) I never saw myself wearing a "big dress" on my wedding day; I was drawn to the flapper style and that's the route I went down.

What do you love most about the dress? The beadwork. It's a reproduction of an original 1920s dress. I also thought the car wash hem was fun.

Wedding décor and details I collected all the vintage china myself (www.vintageteasets.co.uk) and had teacup candles everywhere as well. We were on a budget, but luckily our wedding venue was full of character, so, apart from some little touches here and there, it didn't need much. We used lots of fairy lights, and I had some old medicine bottles and popped cardboard fairies in them—inspired by the Cottingley fairies of the 1920s. I also raided my house for anything that could be used as fun props. We chose our favorite books from the 1920s and early 30s and made hanging notices and table names out of them. *The Great Gatsby* is one of my favorites, quintessentially Roaring Twenties, and for Adam, who is a lover of science fiction, *Brave New World*. Although we went for a 1920s look, it wasn't meant to be an actual theme. However the guests really did get in the spirit and turned up in full-on 20s style, which was a lovely surprise. It especially made for a fun evening when we had the band playing the Charleston, as everyone got into the swing.

Advice for other brides who love 1920s style? There are lots of beautiful 1920s-style replica dresses out there now—plenty of choices—so have a good look around.

The 1930s

The 1930s is my favorite era. I am in love with the silver-screen glamour of it all, and those elegant red carpet gowns. It was my era of choice when it came to styling my own vintage-inspired wedding.

A decade of extravagance in the 1920s was followed by a decade of economic struggle on a worldwide scale in the 1930s, following the Wall Street Crash of 1929 and the subsequent Great Depression. To help lift the spirits of downtrodden nations, huge investment was made in Hollywood productions to entertain the masses and create a sense of escapism. American cinema and cinematic costume design had a huge impact on bridal fashion of the time. Iconic stars such as Garbo, Hayworth, and Dietrich led the way, influencing everything from clothing, hairstyles, and even the way makeup was applied.

Encouraged by new bridal magazines, what we know today as the wedding boutique was being established in major towns and cities. Department stores were also starting to stock ready-to-wear wedding dresses and hosting wedding shows for prospective brides—these were rich pickings for department store owners, who were also establishing the first wedding gift list services.

The bridal trousseau was still a fashionable concept in the 1930s. The popularity of the trousseau has faded with time, but in the 1930s it would typically contain several items of clothing, including a going away outfit, evening gowns, hats, gloves—the wealthier bride's trousseau would also include beautiful jewelry and furs. (Wallis Simpson's was said to contain 40 hats—that's some fancy trousseau!). A modern-day trousseau is a wonderful way to really engage with the spirit of an age gone by; fill it with more practical items such as a pretty frock to wear on your honeymoon, some lovely jewelry, or perfume.

Dress style best suited to:
a tall, slim frame, but also suits natural curves beautifully.

Key bridal looks of the period:
- Hollywood glamour
- Silk bias-cut dresses
- Slinky, draped, flowing fabric
- Floor-sweeping gowns and long languid lines
- Art Deco accents
- Elegance and sophistication—return to a more feminine look
- Close-fitting cloche hat headpieces
- Tiaras
- Long "leg o' mutton" sleeves
- Dresses featuring very little embellishment
- Large, hooped underskirt gowns
- Rhinestone jewelry
- Fur wraps/stoles

VINTAGE INSPIRATION

Left: William (Jock) Alves and Nancy Hart, 1932, Edinburgh, Scotland. The bride wore a full-length bias-cut dress.

Above: A stunningly elegant photograph of a bride, her bridesmaid, and her pageboy, on her wedding day in Rome, Italy, 1934.

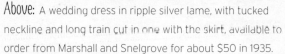

Above: A wedding dress in ripple silver lame, with tucked neckline and long train cut in one with the skirt, available to order from Marshall and Snelgrove for about $50 in 1935.

Top right: Early 1930s bridal fashion was reminiscent of 20s style. This is my Uncle Harold, who wed Ada in August 1930.

Right: Princess Dmitri of Russia in a Chanel wedding dress and veil, with a circlet of orange blossom at the neck, 1932.

FASHION

Even though the invention of Rayon fabric in the 1920s meant that luxury dresses could be manufactured more cost effectively and were therefore cheaper, during the Depression many brides did not have the budget for a new wedding gown, so they chose to wear their Sunday best instead. As a result, aside from the ubiquitous white or ivory, pale pinks and blues, especially, were also popular—possibly inspired by the beautiful pale blue wedding dress worn by Wallis Simpson for her marriage to the Duke of Windsor in 1937.

Brides from families that could afford a wedding dressed elegantly. The boyish silhouettes of the previous decade were discarded for a far more slender, feminine, and glamorous look. There were no corsets, no sack-like dresses; gowns were created in silks that molded to the skin. Waists were nipped in and diamond paneling accentuated curves. Fabric cut on the bias draped beautifully everywhere it needed to, creating an elegant silhouette that looks as fabulous today as it did back then. This is perhaps why so many brides today, some without even realising it, are choosing dresses that were inspired by the glamour of the 30s.

The sleek, floor length, bias-cut look remained the look of the day for most brides right up until the end of the decade, when a new style started to emerge, influenced by the popularity of the film *Gone with the Wind* and its huge gowns with hooped underskirts.

Original 1930s gowns are quite easy to get a hold of via vintage dress supplier specialists. The ones that have survived the test of time will typically feature long buttoned sleeves that billow at the top and taper down to the wrist, or pretty shoulder detailing. Capped sleeves also started to appear during this time—they would often be pleated or ruffled. Most dresses used press studs or looped "rouleau" buttons as fasteners, although the designer Elsa Schiaparelli made use of the zipper in her gowns in the 30s. Dresses in the 30s often had lines of metal buttons sewn very closely together, not only to secure the dress at the back, but to add detail to the sleeves too.

The dresses available now are likely to be very small, so always try before you buy, or check to see if adjustments can be made. Remember that any experienced dressmaker will be able to replicate 1930s designs to fit you perfectly. Bridalwear designers today, whose designs are influenced by the 1930s, include Jenny Packham, Johanna Johnson, Peter Langner, Claire Pettibone, Circa Vintage Brides, and the Vintage Wedding Dress Company.

The cathedral-length wedding veil was still a key piece of the bridal ensemble, though traditional lace veils were being replaced with tulle versions. You can purchase 100% silk lace veils today but they are harder to come by. A fabulous veil designer who specializes in using silk is Ann Guise.

Top Tip

Brides favoring the sleek, bias-cut gowns made fashionable in the 1930s would be wise to invest in lingerie that flattens any little bumps or lumps. Spanx are a godsend—trust me!

The popular floral circlets of the 1920s were still worn but were largely being replaced by tiaras, which became not only a new way of accessorising, but of securing silk tulle veils in place. Tiaras could also be converted into necklaces; they were hugely popular by the mid-point of the decade. They were more than just beautiful adornments, they symbolized the rite of passage from single woman to married bride. Original tiaras can be purchased via vintage jewelry specialists, and there are many designers who specialize in creating vintage-inspired tiaras and headpieces.

The cloche hats of the 20s remained popular during this decade, but another style to emerge was the turban—it allowed women to look chic without having to spend money on having their hair styled to perfection. Vivien Sheriff (www.viviensheriff.co.uk), who has supplied headpieces for the Duchess of Cambridge, has produced a beautiful collection of vintage-inspired headpieces for brides which includes a turban. Be daring, be different, and don a glamorous turban; that is embellished with jewels on your wedding day and you will pull off truly authentic wow factor!

For the perfect pair of 1930s-style heels, look to designers like Emmy (www.emmyshoes.co.uk) or Rachel Simpson (www.rachelsimpsonshoes.co.uk), who both ship overseas. These two designers are heavily influenced by the fashions of the 1920s and 1930s.

To finish off your glamorous look, you might want to consider purchasing a sparkling clutch bag—these are readily available both as original vintage items or modern-day replicas. Pearl studs or chandelier-style earrings infuenced by Art Deco shapes look beautiful in a 30s-inspired bride. Jeweled accessories were an important feature of the bridal look in the 1930s, in order to complement the clean lines and uncluttered, elegant silhouettes of the day. Rhinestone jewelry was very prevalent, and modern-day vintage replicas still make for a beautiful design statement.

It was fashionable to complete the bridal look with fur wraps and jackets; women wanted to look and feel as glamorous

as possible. There are many online shops that specialize in the sale of original vintage furs dating back to the 30s. If original fur isn't your thing, many modern designers are incorporating faux fur into their collections.

Opposite left: Original 1930s silk bias-cut wedding dress by Unforgettable Bridal Gowns.

Opposite right: A selection of 30s-style headpieces incorporating original vintage elements, by Sheena Holland.

Above left: The "Eva" shoes by Emmy feature a T-bar with Art Deco-style embellishment.

Above right: A fringe tiara by Sheena Holland designed to be worn over the front of the head. This reworked tiara made from vintage baguette-shaped diamanté is not for the faint hearted.

Wedding bouquets in the 30s continued to feature mostly white blooms, but, unless her family was wealthy, most brides simply could not afford a bouquet and used locally-grown flowers instead. The shower bouquet of the 1920s, which cascaded with ribbons and flowers almost to the ground, was still a popular style. Brides also opted for smaller posies that could be held by just one hand—the stems would be wrapped in ribbon or fabric and studded with pearls or beads. Long-stem calla lilies made an ideal bloom for a bouquet that

was traditionally carried across the arm. Roses were also popular. Another distinct style to emerge in the 30s was the "nosegay." This was a more rounded bouquet with flowers closely packed together, and it featured lots of greenery.

Above: A contemporary take on the classic large bouquets of the 30s by the Real Cut Flower Garden, here using delicate garden flowers including astrantia and clematis with peonies and ivies.

Left: The exquisite hand-sequinned "Erte" cape by the State of Grace. A glamorous addition to any 30s-inspired wedding wardrobe.

Opposite: Original vintage fur cape from Vintage Fur Hire.

THE 1930S BRIDE

Sarah wears a bias-cut gown of Amalfi satin and silk tulle called "Sarah Jane" by designer Jacqueline Byrne for Luella's Boudoir. The low-cut neckline and cowl detail in the back evoke a sense of 1930s red carpet glamour.

Here, Sarah wears a 1930s-inspired champagne silk dress featuring the bias-cut diamond paneling so typical of the era. It molds to the body and the seam lines give a fabulous hourglass shape. The belt cinches in at a high waist (usually the thinnest part of a woman). The high neckline is flattering, as the darts over the bust help give shape, and it unveils just a hint of collarbone. So many 30s dresses showed very little flesh but had a sexy perfume-bottle silhouette. The belt, created by Cherished Vintage using Art Deco dress embellishments, brings gentle sparkle and definition to the waist. The look is completed with a beautiful necklace, crafted from vintage elements by Victoria Millésime, and a vintage-style lace and freshwater pearl bridal cap, by the same designer.

BEAUTY

By the 1930s, cosmetics had become a multimillion dollar industry. It was, in fact, the only industry to progress and expand during the Great Depression. Makeup became the required essential for all well-groomed women, who were inspired by their glamorous on-screen idols.

Brands such as Max Factor and Elizabeth Arden were firmly established during this period, and they produced everything from the perfect indelible lipstick to false eyelashes. Smouldering advertising campaigns encouraged women to invest in powder, lipstick, brow pencils, and eyeshadow; some shouted "Matching lips and finger-tips are the new sensation," while others featured couples in romantic embraces.

Red lipstick was the choice of most women in the 1930s. I believe there is a shade of red lipstick for everyone and would encourage brides to experiment with various shades—it adds a beautiful touch of glamour on your wedding day.

If strong red isn't your thing and you still want to pull off a glamorous 30s-style look, try working with a paler pink lip shade.

Eyes were smouldering. A smoky eye is a great look with a paler lipstick (red or pink). Alternatively, keep the eyes tamer, lining them with kohl, and focus on a redder lip.

In my opinion, a 30s hairstyle that will never date and that works well on both short and long hair is the marvelous Marcel wave. It was a similar look to the finger waves of the 1920s; only the technique of achieving the look differentiated it. Many old Hollywood starlets, including Marlene Dietrich, Bette Davis, Greta Garbo, and Joan Crawford, assisted in making both the pin curl and Marcel hugely appealing to women all over the world. This elegant hairstyle had actually been pioneered some decades earlier by French coiffeur Francois Marcel Grateau but, thanks to the invention of heated curling irons in the 1930s, the graceful look was easier to achieve than ever before. Again, it's a tricky style to achieve and should always be left to a professional hairstylist; but book a trial run with them first, as not all stylists are skilled enough to master this look.

Women were investing in their nails too, and matching them to their lip color. Go for a striking deep red nail varnish on your wedding day in keeping with this vintage trend. Or try something truly eye-catching like a black varnish, which was also popular for a while in the 30s.

Opposite: A red lip typifies the glamorous look many women sought during the 1930s.

Right: The fabulous Marcel wave, made popular by many silver-screen icons of the time. It could be worn long, as seen in the top image, or pinned under for a sleek, neat look.

DÉCOR AND DETAILS

Style was all about unadulterated glamour in the 1930s and cinema ruled the day. Evoking this sense of high-fashion glamour and elegance is easy on a wedding day. What other day do you get the opportunity to dress up in the finest gown you will probably ever purchase, after all?

The Art Deco movement was still strong and its motifs can be incorporated into cake and stationery design. Drawing inspiration from the beaded embellishments that were so fashionable in the Deco period, the cake design opposite reflects the more feminine and glamorous 30s. Think of the films of the Golden Age of Hollywood and you'll get an idea of the sparkling, sophisticated style.

The Art Deco-inspired mirrored stationery on page 61, created by Cutture (www.cutture.com), features laser-cut, handwritten details and represents the essence of the 1930s "boudoir bride."

The idea of the "boudoir bride" can be further incorporated into your wedding by using boudoir-like elements, such as mirrored pieces of furniture and accessories. Use old props that suggest a boudoir scene to style an area where your guests can leave cards and gifts. Drape pearls over an old dressing table and decorate it with beautiful flowers and vintage perfume bottles—pull the drawers open and have the blooms spilling and trailing out of them.

A wedding venue can play a huge role in setting the desired period effect. Do your research and look for beautiful examples of original Art Deco architecture for a ready-made, glamorous vintage backdrop.

HERE ARE SOME CULTURAL REFERENCES TO INSPIRE YOU:

- Golden Age of Hollywood
- Red carpet glamour
- Stars of the silver screen: Marlene Dietrich, Jean Harlow, Greta Garbo, Bette Davis, Joan Crawford, Fred Astaire, Ginger Rogers, Cary Grant, Clark Gable
- Famous musicians: Bing Crosby, Duke Ellington, Glen Miller, Billie Holiday, Ella Fitzgerald
- The "boudoir bride" look
- Popular literature of the time: Agatha Christie's *Poirot*, F. Scott Fitzgerald's *Tender Is the Night*, Aldous Huxley's *Brave New World*
- Black and white tie for the gentlemen
- Gramophone records
- Film: *Gone with the Wind*

When it comes to entertaining your guests in authentic 30s style, consider hiring a romantic singer to perform songs from the time. Many use authentic backing tracks so you get the unmistakable sound and feel of the big-band era without the hassle or expense of hiring a full band. Have a slow smooch on the dance floor or sip away on elegantly-named cocktails as your guests do the same.

Above: Annabel of vintage gramophone-playing duo It's a Windup!

Right: A beautiful vintage atomizer perfume bottle. Scour antique stores for originals or purchase replica bottles to help style your wedding reception.

Alternatively, if you want to have a more lively atmosphere, find a specialist vintage gramophone player; there are companies out there who will play vintage shellac 78s for a truly authentic sound. See the Suppliers section at the back of the book for some of my favorite performers.

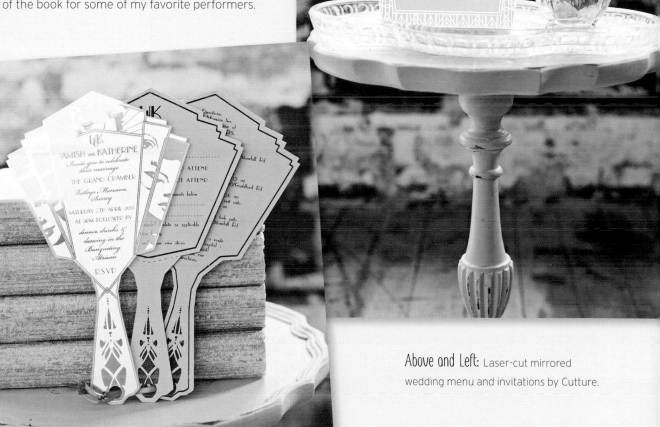

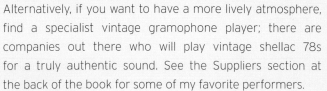

Above and Left: Laser-cut mirrored wedding menu and invitations by Cutture.

REAL BRIDE

HANNAH & FREDDIE'S WEDDING
JUNE 4, 2011

Dress An original 1930s vintage wedding dress from Heavenly Vintage Brides (www.heavenlyvintagebrides.co.uk).

Headpiece Bespoke using antique flowers by Rosie Weisencrantz (www.rosieweisencrantz.com).

Accessories The necklace was an antique that my mother wore on her wedding day, a present from my grandmother, her mother-in-law—it was both my "something borrowed" and "blue." The clutch bag was original 20s/early-30s and the sunglasses were 70s, both from Belle Amie Vintage.

Shoes Modern.

What inspired you to wear a beautiful original 1930s wedding dress? I have always loved vintage things as well as seeking out something that feels just right and just me. I wanted something that tied me to the tradition of weddings, back through the past and to another bride and the commitment she made, not to a cast of modern brides picking from the same designers.

What do you love most about the dress? I love the train and the glamour of it. And I love that I have a photograph of the original bride wearing it on her own wedding day.

Do you have any advice for other brides who are looking to recreate this kind of look? Mix it up. Unless you want to literally recreate an era and theme accordingly, add things from every era. I had Victorian jewelry, 70s shades, and my nails were gold metallic by Minx to add an edge. And collect as you go: garage sales, secondhand shops, your parents attic, etc. It's really fun. I'd also really recommend finding suppliers you enjoy talking to and who understand what you want from your outfit/look/day without you having to overexplain.

REAL BRIDE

SOPHIE & BARNEY'S WEDDING
OCTOBER 22, 2010

Dress Original 30s dress from stylist Zoe Lem (www.zoelem.co.uk).

Accessories Original vintage silver fox fur coat, on loan from my mom—a gift from my dad when she gave birth to me! Lilly Lewis headpiece (www.lillylewis.co.uk) and a vintage brooch.

What inspired you to wear a beautiful original 1930s dress? I wanted an heirloom that I could pass down. I love anything that has a bit of a history to it, and the typical 1930s silhouette was all I had in mind: long sleeves, silk-covered buttons, and cut on the bias. Plus I wanted to have a good time at my wedding and dance, so I didn't want any corseting or boning. It felt like a second skin and the color was perfect. It was the only wedding dress I ever tried on! I went to Zoe looking for bridesmaid's hats and happened to describe what I wanted for myself. She brought out the dress, beautifully sculpted and absolutely perfect. It just needed some restoration. Pure destiny!

What do you love most about the dress? The detail on the back, the seams, the silk-covered buttons and panel details; you just wouldn't find that level of detail with a repro dress, only an authentic one. I can't believe I was going to chop off the train so that I could dance in it better! In the end I couldn't bear to change one thing about such an old piece, so I left it, and I'm so glad I did because it made the whole thing so dramatic. I love that it's almost sheer because the fabric is ninety years old. I loved that it was quite sexy, as it clung to every curve, but I was still covered up.

Wedding décor and details Together Barney and I designed, built, and printed everything ourselves. Barney hung the vintage chandeliers and dressed the venue, and I created the print-based stuff, like cameos for the seats and the personalized Penguin book covers. My lovely mom and all her friends covered one hundred thrift shop books (one for each guest) with the covers.

Advice for other brides who love 1930s style? Everything was generally old, faded, and worn, from the dress and invite paper, down to the faded-looking roses I had for my bouquet. For a genuine look, I would always recommend going for real vintage instead of reproduction when it's possible and don't be a slave to a theme. Throw in everything you and your partner love and then you'll get a really organic look that's truly personal to you both.

The 1940s

By the time the 1940s had arrived, the world was at war again. Many weddings during this period were hastily planned to occur during military leave. Couples often had as little as forty-eight hours in which to plan their weddings and get married. It is difficult to imagine what it must have been like for brides of the time—so many traditional wedding customs taken for granted in the past were simply not allowed—even the sound of church bells was reserved to alert citizens of a potential enemy attack.

While families tried to ensure that weddings were jolly occasions, high-end glamour took a backseat during the 40s. The production of lace was halted during the war, and silk was predominantly used to produce military parachutes—leaving both fabrics scarce. Silk-like rayon and satin were widely used instead.

In the United Kingdom, ration books were issued to every citizen and included coupons for clothing and even footwear. Brides were given extra coupons for their wedding and they would save these and utilize ones kindly donated by family and friends to purchase a wedding dress. But wedding dresses were in scarce supply for most and those available were more expensive than usual; many brides simply couldn't afford the number of coupons required. As a result, most brides had to "make-do-and-mend." They learned to be creative, either borrowing and refashioning gowns from family or friends, or making dresses using spare pieces of fabric, which may have included items like curtain netting.

Some brides continued to enjoy traditional white weddings, but it was considered by many to be unpatriotic to marry in a big white gown during the war years. Many brides chose to marry in wartime utility clothing, simple crêpe daytime dresses or a "wedding suit" which comprised a narrow, knee-length skirt and jacket—often in military style and, if the bride could afford it, accessorised with a pair of seamed nylon stockings.

Dress style best suited to:
the more curvaceous "hourglass" figure.

Key bridal looks of the period:
- Broad shoulders, often featuring epaulettes
- Dresses made from crêpe, rayon, and satin
- Military/utility-style wedding suits (narrow skirt and jacket)
- Smaller wedding bouquets or posies
- Sweetheart and V-shaped necklines
- Draped jersey
- Peplums
- Light shoulder padding
- "Something borrowed"
- Elaborate hats and headpieces

VINTAGE INSPIRATION

Above: A silk A-line "Princess" gown with a long train and full-length tapered sleeves. The photograph was taken in 1947—on the very cusp of Dior's New Look. The war had ended and spare parachute silk was being used to fashion wedding dresses. Brides could afford to invest more in their gown and focus on the luxury they had to set aside during the war.

Above: This bride, photographed in 1945, wears a full-length gown with a puddle train and peplum waist. Peplums were hugely popular in the 40s, evident in collections by the likes of Chanel and Dior, and continue in popularity today – they flatter the figure by creating an hourglass silhouette.

Right: These are my grandparents, Norman and Edna Bailey on their wedding day in November 1942, Lichfield, England. Grandma wore a "wedding suit," comprising a narrow skirt and jacket. She told me before she passed away that she purchased the suit so that she could wear it again.

Above left: Len and Irene Bruce, March 1948 – Irene's wedding dress, bouquet, and veil are typical 40s style.

Above right: Marriage of the Hon. Deborah Vivien Freeman-Mitford to Andrew Cavendish, later the Duke of Devonshire, in 1941. The bride wore a dress by Victor Stiebel.

FASHION

Fashion has a habit of following changes in society, and the huge changes taking place across the globe during World War II were soon to impact bridal trends, fashion, and weddings in general.

There are many vintage wedding dresses from the 40s that have survived the test of time beautifully, and can be purchased via specialist suppliers. They will tend to feature less embellishment than their glamorous counterparts of the previous decades; with everyone conscripted to work for the war, there just wasn't time to spend hours hand-embellishing wedding gowns. Bridal fashion took on a more modest look: necks, arms, and backs were covered and trains were short, so the bridal fashion of this era is probably more suited to those who prefer a less glitzy, more understated look.

If you do fall in love with an original 1940s wedding dress but feel it's missing something special, consider accessorizing it with some pretty dress clips or ask a dressmaker to sew in some embellishment. Alternatively, finish your look with beautiful vintage jewelry or a clutch bag.

Dress shades included snow white, ivory, blush, and champagne, and often featured full-length sleeves—the sleeves themselves being gathered and more roomy towards the top, with shoulders featuring some light padding. You can always have any padding removed if you prefer.

This silhouette, along with a pretty sweetheart neckline and gathering around the bodice, created an illusion of a smaller waist. Look out for dresses with pretty peplum details around the waist too, another popular design feature of the time.

If you want to pull off a truly authentic 40s look, consider opting for a modern interpretation of a 40s-style utility suit —done right, this look can be incredibly chic and elegant on the modern-day bride. Let's face it, a big fancy wedding dress isn't for everyone. Utilize either the darker military colors or abandon these for something more modern and contemporary—even ivory. Talk to a dressmaker and ask them to share fabric samples with you.

A seamed stocking would look fabulous with a skirt suit. For a modern twist on the steamed stocking, visit What Katie Did (www.whatkatiedid.com) or, for something a little more extravagant, try Bebaroque (www.bebaroque.com), who specialize in the design of embellished and embroidered leg-wear. Unworn or excellent condition preworn original vintage, full-fashioned seamed stockings (designed in the shape of the leg) can still be purchased. I have a pair of unworn stockings in this style that my mom picked up at an auction for me for next to nothing.

The 1940s bridal outfit was often finished off with an elaborate hat and matching accessories, such as a handbag and small

posy of flowers. A bride would often carry a lucky horseshoe charm, like my grandma did in the image on page 69. This goodluck accessory might often be the only giveaway that its owner was actually a bride.

A wonderful alternative to a traditional flower bouquet is a vintage jewelry bouquet. This is made up of entirely original jewelry pieces in the shape of a bouquet. It can also feature other accessories, such as pearls and feathers. This type of bouquet is becoming more popular nowadays and, while it makes an authentic nod to the past, it can also be preserved as a beautiful heirloom for the future. You can make your own, but visit the Suppliers section at the back of this book to discover companies who specialize in creating this type of bouquet.

Headpieces tended to be high, mimicking crown designs and featured stiff lace, wax flowers, and beading. Veils tended to be shorter, to reflect the more austere times. Other headpieces that became popular in the 40s included

a coronet-style tiara—possibly inspired by the marriage of Queen Elizabeth to Prince Philip of Greece in 1947. For smaller, but just as exquisite, 40s-inspired headpieces, take a look at The Romance Collection by Scottish designer Renee Walrus, which was created to reflect 1940s Hollywood glamour inspired by the style icons Veronica Lake and Rita Hayworth (www.renewalrus.co.uk).

Short wedding gloves ending at the wrist were a popular choice. Cornelia James (www.corneliajames.com) has a wide variety of beautiful lace gloves, or try the fabulous online bridal store BHLDN (www.bhldn.com).

Shoes worn by brides with dresses would have either been already owned or borrowed, but there are some lovely original 1940s shoes available through speciality vintage sellers today that suggest the mid-heeled, slingback, open toe style was popular—often with a single bar. They come in gold and silver, and look almost like a pair of professional dancing shoes. These can be purchased for a very reasonable

Did you know that as rations were still in place when the Queen tied the knot? Many thousands of loyal citizens sent their ration coupons to Buckingham Palace as a contribution towards the Queen's wedding dress.

price from sellers, and their heel height will mean your feet shouldn't feel too crippled by the end of a long day dancing and socializing with guests. The designer Rachel Simpson (www.rachelsimpsonshoes.co.uk) has some lovely vintage-inspired heels; the kitty design would be particularly suited to a 40s-style bride.

Finish off an authentic look with a vintage fur or faux fur coat to add a sense of glamour.

Although rations extended for several years after the end of the war in 1945, once the war was over, most brides returned to wearing white for their wedding and sought the bridal glamour of times gone by. This perfectly coincided with the launch of Christian Dior's luxurious New Look, with its voluptuous hourglass silhouette and tiny nipped-in waists, which would go on to have a huge influence on bridal fashion in the 40s and 50s. Look for vintage dresses with corseted waists and more rounded shoulders and long, full skirts—the make-do-and-mend ethos was being left behind for a new style of glamour. Queen Elizabeth II married in 1947 and her wedding dress, reminiscent of the bridal silhouette that had been influenced by Dior, inspired many brides.

Opposite: A beautiful alternative to flowers—a vintage jewelry bouquet by designer Basia Zarzycka that incorporates original vintage elements such as beads, pearls, and crystals.

Top: Original vintage bridal gloves and accessories.

Right: Keep accessories simple and fuss-free for a 1940s look.

THE 1940S BRIDE

Ivana is wearing a design by Circa Vintage Brides (www.circabrides.com). This beautiful 1940s dress features the signature silhouette of the era, nipping in high above the waistline, which is very flattering. It is a glamorous Hollywood style with the wide neckline, neat waist, and long A-line skirt shape.

Here, Ivana wears a modern-day, vintage-inspired design by Zoe Lem (www.zoelem.co.uk). Although in many ways a less formal dress than the big structured wedding gowns typically worn by women during this period, this 1940s-inspired dress has a very simple but clever way of flattering the figure. The pintucks are a beautiful way of nipping in the waist and form an hourglass silhouette in a not-so-obvious manner. The one-piece sleeve offers gentle gathering around the arm and creates a soft shoulder that highlights the waist detail even more. The A-line skirt is very flattering and gives balance to the shoulders. It is the attention to detail that is so beautiful in so many vintage patterns.

BEAUTY

Regardless of everything that was happening, women still did their very best to look good during the war. To maintain their morale, women purchased makeup and cosmetic products whenever they could, even though the supply was limited. Lipstick came to represent a symbol of femininity, and red lipstick ruled the look of the day; other aspects of makeup were kept to a more natural, pared-down look.

One very popular shade of red in the 1940s erred towards orange. Try the fabulous Lady Danger shade by MAC lipstick to recreate this look now (this shade is only available in the larger MAC stores).

The pencil thin eyebrow look of the 30s was replaced with a fuller brow but a well-plucked and pronounced long arch. It was also desirable to have a rosy glow skin complexion, with a gentle hint of rouge on the cheeks.

It was all about the lashes too; lashes would have been long, so make the most of the false lashes available today or consider having a set of semipermanent lashes applied in time for your wedding day. The added bonus of semipermanents is that you can skip the mascara for the day and not worry too much about runny eye makeup! I can't recommend them enough. Your local beauty salon will be able to advise.

Right: Red lipstick ruled the beauty scene in the 1940s.

While even Hollywood played down fashion during the early half of the decade, the 1940s produced several icons who heavily influenced how women styled their hair and makeup, including Rita Hayworth, Vivien Leigh, Betty Grable, Lana Turner, and Veronica Lake. These were the "bombshell" screen sirens of the day.

Most women had shoulder-length or longer hair in the 1940s and tended to pile it high on top of their heads, curling it using old-fashioned boudoir techniques like wet rags.

The peekaboo hairstyle made famous by Veronica Lake is a fab 40s look. Typically parted to the side and featuring large seductive waves, the side opposite the parting is styled to cascade seductively into the face, gently concealing the eye (hence the term peekaboo). This particular style will suit brides today who have medium to long hair, who wish to wear their hair down but maintain a glamorous look.

For those who really want to wear their hair up, a popular up-do that emerged in the 40s was the Victory Roll. Victory Rolls were more of a practical style—designed to keep hair away from the munitions machinery that many women would be operating during the war. Ask your hair stylist to experiment with a modern, elegant twist, á la Dita Von Teese. The Victory Roll will give away your love of the 40s vintage style in an instant. It is a true signature look of the era and can be easily fashioned to wear alongside a veil or headpiece.

For painted nails, pretty much any color was suitable, as long as it corresponded with what you were wearing—any shade of pink or red, even blue!

DÉCOR AND DETAILS

The 1940s offers a haven of inspiration for the bride who loves to DIY; the homemade look was prevalent and this can be applied to all styling elements of a wedding day.

Opting for a marquee over a more glamorous traditional hotel reception will help add to the authenticity of your 40s-inspired wedding. Get your guests involved in the spirit of the times by creating a delicious table buffet. You can pick up trestle tables fairly cheaply at places like Ikea, then style them with freshly-picked flowers in jars and vintage tablecloths (this would be a lovely task to pass on to your bridesmaids). For your wedding cake, ask a close relative or friend to bake a big Victoria sponge cake and layer it with fresh fruit, strawberries, and cream. Or, instead of a single cake, invite those guests that can bake to bring along their own homemade cakes, biscuits, or sweet treats. This "everyone helping out" style of reception will mirror the street parties that would have taken place in the 40s, particularly during national celebratory events.

Some brides may have grandparents who were alive during the war. Speak to them about what it was like. Ask if they have any old items that could be used at your wedding or plunder your local thrift shops and garage sales, seeking out old suitcases, patriotic paraphernalia, tassled lamps, tea sets and vases, vintage typewriters, oil lamps, old fruit crates, books, etc.

Model your wedding stationery after wartime telegrams or love letters to sweethearts. Use postcards or luggage tags as place settings. Decorate tables with original vintage postcards featuring romantic scenes; these can usually be picked up at thrift shops or vintage stores for very little. Designer Vicky Trainor of the Vintage Drawer crafts the most delightful gifts, wedding favors, reception signage, and table décor using vintage fabrics. Each piece is individually handmade, making it completely unique (see examples on page 83).

HERE ARE SOME CULTURAL REFERENCES TO INSPIRE YOU:

- Keep it homegrown/homebaked
- Make-do-and-mend—be resourceful and DIY
- Something borrowed
- Military styling
- Patriotism
- Film stars: Betty Grable, Lauren Bacall, Veronica Lake, Rita Hayworth, Humphrey Bogart, Cary Grant
- Singers and musicans: Billie Holiday, Frank Sinatra, Ella Fitzgerald, Gracie Fields
- Swingtime jazz, big band, and bebop
- Street parties and marquees

Mr & Mrs Fraser Clearie
request the pleasure of the company of

Oliver & Violet

to join them in celebrating the
marriage of their daughter,

Lorna Helen
to
Cédric Orgeret

at Alloway Parish Church
on Monday 15th July 2013 at 2.30pm
and afterwards at Brig o'Doon House Hotel.

RSVP by 1st March
5 Waterfern Lane
Kilbarchan
Renfrewshire
PA10 2HF
Scotland

To ensure an authentic 1940s look, use seasonal flowers and different styles of blooms to achieve an eclectic effect. Large bouquets were considered frivolous, hence the more popular posy-style bouquet of the time. Many brides in the 40s opted for a simple corsage worn either around the wrist or across the lapel of a wedding suit jacket. Pick flowers fresh from your garden or buy them from a local florist the day before your wedding and then style them in any suitable container you can find, including old tins, jam jars, and vases. These can all be decorated with ribbon, burlap, buttons, or any other pretty accessory.

In an effort to raise spirits, music tended to be upbeat and jazzy in the 1940s. Delight your guests into a celebratory swing and jive by hiring a swing band or orchestra. You'll have your guests merrily singing and doing the boogie woogie in no time.

Opposite: A selection of wartime correspondence-inspired wedding stationery, created by Artcadia.

Above: A pair of bride and groom chair signs and a wedding day menu, each crafted from vintage tablecloths and other linens by Vicky Trainor of the Vintage Drawer.

LUCY & JOHN'S WEDDING
MAY 14, 2011

Dress Original 1940s silk crêpe dress, with 30s/40s dress clips sewn onto the cuffs and an original bow brooch attached to the back of the dress.

Accessories The headpiece was from the mall and the bouquet of vintage jewelry and buttons I made myself.

Shoes High street ballet pumps, accessorized with 1940s dress clips and flower buttons.

What inspired you to wear a beautiful 1940s wedding dress? I knew I wanted a vintage dress. I had envisaged myself in a 1950s number, but absolutely fell in love when I stumbled across this gem in a really tiny, dark vintage clothes shop in Covent Garden. The shop was so small that you couldn't see how long the train was. The dress didn't fit me (I couldn't do up the back at all), but I just loved it. I decided it would be worth coming back the next day, and I spent half the night with my mom talking about how we could make it fit.

The next day, we discovered that the WHOLE dress was covered in brown foxing marks and I was devastated. I couldn't afford to buy a dress with stains that might not come out, and so, brokenheartedly, left it at the shop where the owner said she might clean it. But a week later I got a call from the owner saying that she'd cleaned the dress and it was perfect. Mom did the most amazing job on it, repairing the few holes in the train, letting out the sleeves, taking out the zipper and creating a backless effect, without cutting away any of the fabric. We tried to keep it in as original a state as possible, so if anyone ever wanted to wear it again with a closed back, they'd have enough fabric to do so.

What do you love most about the dress? The fact that my mom did such an amazing job of repairing it and making it backless, followed by the train, the beading, and the shoulders!

Wedding décor and details We borrowed and crafted pretty much all the details for the big day, and when it was all thrown together, it had a 40s vibe to it. I scoured thrift shops for vintage plates and teacups and we raided my parents' loft for accessories to dress the reception venue: candlesticks, photo frames, vases, a mini Fortnum & Mason hamper, vintage suitcases, old books, etc. We made bunting at my bachelorette party to use on the day and my mom made the confetti out of flowers from home. We made our own programs using vintage typography and graphics we sourced online. I also made a family tree by framing and displaying the wedding photos of both our families, which was a lovely talking point. And instead of a traditional guest book, we collected vintage postcards and invited each guest to choose one and write messages to us on them.

We rented champagne saucers, rather than flutes, to achieve that elegant vintage feel and took our own gramophone (and our friend brought his along too) to the drinks reception. Finally, a friend acted as chauffeur for us with his vintage Land Rover.

Do you have any advice for other brides who are looking to recreate this kind of look? Don't take your prospective husband to wedding fairs! Bargain hunt at thrift shops, jumble sales, and auctions. Don't be afraid to throw together things from different eras—just choose things that appeal and are meaningful to you. I can honestly say that everything at our wedding was something we cherished, either because it was linked to loved ones, or because of the excitement of how we found it. It's not about spending lots of money.

The 1950s

The 1950s was a period of optimism, hope, and prosperity and a time of wondrous new inventions, fashions, fads, and technology. Emphasis was placed on the family and home; advertising campaigns targeting women encouraged them to consider the role of housewife as a career, and marriage was idealized in the media. A new pop culture was emerging too: rock 'n' roll became a defining sound of the era. Youth culture embraced this new musical genre. Girls dressed up in full-circle skirts, neat fitting tops, and stilettos and tied their hair in ponytails; boys slicked their hair into prominent forelocks and donned Teddy Boy suits and winklepickers—think of the musical *Grease* and you'll get the picture!

Developments in fashion reflected the huge changes taking place across society. This was led predominantly by Dior's New Look—a nipped-in, strong hourglass silhouette—which was to have a huge influence on the design of bridalwear. Other high-fashion designers whose work inspired bridal fashion included Balenciaga, Givenchy, and Pierre Balmain.

Cinema stars also still held sway; the original *Father of the Bride* film, featuring Elizabeth Taylor, spawned thousands of copies of the wedding dress worn by Taylor's character Katherine Banks, and the bateau-neck, full-circle dress worn by Audrey Hepburn in the film *Funny Face* was copied over and over again. Celebrity weddings exuding high society glamour included those of Elizabeth Taylor, Grace Kelly, and Audrey Hepburn. Jackie Onassis married her beloved John F. Kennedy in 1953, too.

Fifties-inspired bridal fashion has seen a huge resurgence in the past couple of years. I think the fun and playful aspect of this era appeals to many couples today, but also the dress shapes that emerged during this era tend to suit a broad variety of figures and sizes—particularly the fuller figure.

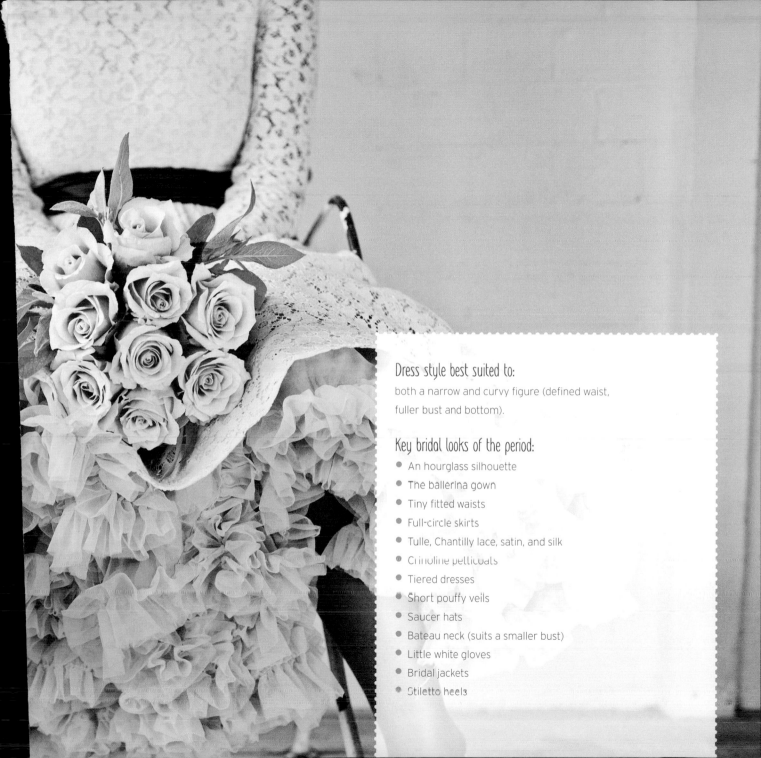

Dress style best suited to:
both a narrow and curvy figure (defined waist, fuller bust and bottom).

Key bridal looks of the period:

- An hourglass silhouette
- The ballerina gown
- Tiny fitted waists
- Full-circle skirts
- Tulle, Chantilly lace, satin, and silk
- Crinoline petticoats
- Tiered dresses
- Short pouffy veils
- Saucer hats
- Bateau neck (suits a smaller bust)
- Little white gloves
- Bridal jackets
- Stiletto heels

VINTAGE INSPIRATION

Above: A classically beautiful dress of embroidered organza foaming over water green faille. This dress was made to order at Harrods Trousseau Room, 1957.

The TATLER

MAY 7, 1958 & BYSTANDER

BRIDE & HOME NUMBER — 2/-

Above: Front cover of *The Tatler*, May 1958 bridal issue.

Opposite top left: This bride is dressed in typical 1950s style – her dress retains an element of modesty, with shoulders covered up and beneath a fitted bodice falls a delightful skirt of tulle and lace. The bride, pictured with her father, is believed to have been one of the original Bluebell dance girls–she married a US Marine.

Top right: A lovely bride prays for a happy wedding day. She wears a long veil and late-50s medieval-style wedding dress with fitted sleeves and a drop waist.

Right: Reg and May Miller on their 1950s wedding day. May wears an early 50s gown, timeless in style—it would look as good today as it did back then.

FASHION

Bridal fashion in the 1950s was dominated by that classic 50s style: a full skirt and nipped-in waist. This style came in several different forms—full length, tea length/ballerina style, bateau neck, narrow sloping shoulders, three-quarter length sleeves, full sleeves, sleeveless, tiers of lace—but the basic silhouette of an hourglass with a tiny waist remained the staple look of the era.

At the start of the decade, modesty was the watchword for brides; shoulders would tend to be covered, sleeves would be three-quarter or full length, and many dresses were worn with matching jackets to preserve modesty at the altar. Bare arms were a no-no for most church ceremonies (look at Grace Kelly's wedding dress for a classic example of 50s modesty-meets-high-fashion glamour). If you're not into the idea of sleeves but likewise don't want to expose too much arm flesh, a cap sleeve either on or off the shoulder (see the dress worn by Jackie Onassis to John F. Kennedy in 1953) will provide some comfort.

Another look to emerge during the 50s was the "Princess Bride." Hepburn's role in *Roman Holiday* was hugely influential; this extravagant style of gown was replicated by many designers of the time and featured huge full skirts, supported beneath by hoops and stiff petticoats of starched tulle or crinoline. Of course, the other princess whose choice of bridal wear was to have a phenomenal impact on bridal

fashion was Grace Kelly, who, on marrying her real-life Prince Charming, dazzled thousands of brides the world over with a beautiful gown that oozed regal glamour. That tight-fitting bodice with long lace sleeves and a large skirt is a look whose popularity has been further emphasized by the wedding of the Duchess of Cambridge to Prince William. While it may not be a look that appeals to all modern-day brides, it is unarguably timeless and elegant.

You'll probably find that most vintage wedding dress suppliers stock more gowns from the 1950s than any other decade. Not only were many more wedding dresses made during this decade to meet demand, many of them were made from fabrics that better stand the test of time, including the synthetic fabric nylon. More expensive wedding dresses were made using lace and duchesse satin. Many of the 50s vintage wedding gowns you may find available today will be fashioned from lace or tulle, which were both hugely popular. Lace with a high cotton content will not yellow over time—check for any discolouration before you buy and always ask if any imperfections can be covered up or restored.

There is something so wonderfully feminine and elegant about 50s wedding dresses that they appeal to many brides today—but be mindful of your body shape. The hourglass silhouette suits many body shapes, particularly those ladies with a fuller figure, but a dress with layer upon layer of tulle

Left: This lovely 1950s dress (restored by Heavenly Vintage Brides) has a boned lace-covered bodice and a skirt of tiered layers of tulle. Like all the best 50s shapes, it gives the appearance of a small waist and enhances the bust.

Below: Structure really came into play in the 50s. This nipped-in dress by Zoe Lem gives a great hourglass shape, and the square neckline would frame the face perfectly.

Opposite: A selection of original 1950s wedding dresses from Elizabeth Avey.

Some may say it's sacrilege to make too many alterations to an original vintage wedding dress, but if a certain aspect of it isn't working for you, seek the advice of a seamstress or specialist alterations company. My advice is to make the dress your own. If this means adding or removing sleeves, or shortening the dress length, do it.

might overwhelm a tiny frame. Also, because the emphasis was on the nipped-in look, many original 50s wedding gowns available today will feature a very small waist, so it is critical you attempt to try an original gown on for fit before committing to buy it. A speciality alterations service may be able to modify a bodice to create a more comfortable fit, but this isn't always possible.

It's important to mention that those tiny waistlines of the 50s were given a helping hand by good corsetry! To create a similar, authentic silhouette, you may want to invest in a modern-day alternative set of underwear. Speak to a lingerie specialist, or even a dressmaker, who will be able to advise you on where to buy a suitable waist-cincher, if required.

Modern designers who are inspired by the 50s include Candy Anthony (www.candyanthony.com), Fancy New York (www.fancybridalny.com), BHLDN (www.bhldn.com), Blue Bridal Wear (www.bluebridalwear.co.uk), Dolly Couture (www.dollycouture.com), and Stephanie Allin (www. stephanieallin.net), and there are many dressmakers who specialize in creating replica gowns. One of my favorite of these designers is Candy Anthony, whose elegant made-to-measure wedding dresses, ball gowns, prom, and evening dresses carry a signature look of glorious full-circle tulle skirts, crafted to the most excellent standards. Designs feature duchesse satins, vintage-inspired lace, soft tulles, and pretty polka-dot overlays. For brides on a tight budget, take a look at Honeypie Boutique (www.honeypieboutique.co.uk)

or Dolly Couture (www.dollycouture.com). Dolly Couture specialize in reproducing the short cocktail and prom-style gowns of the 50s.

As the 1950s progressed, various other bridal styles emerged, including one-shoulder asymmetrical dresses and halterneck designs. Vivien of Holloway in London creates the most fabulous 50s-inspired bridalwear and dresses–their signature look is a full-circle halterneck–and they ship all over the world. Also look up Whirling Turban (www.whirlingturban.com); you send them your measurements and a nifty production unit in Bali sends you a dress!

If traditional white or ivory isn't your preference, try to seek out some original 50s prom gowns. There are many in circulation today that come in a variety of colors and make fabulous wedding dresses for those who prefer not to get married in white. As always, a bespoke dressmaker will be able to replicate this princess/prom style.

When it comes to accessorizing your 50s gown, there is so much opportunity to have fun and be playful! Add layers of petticoats beneath–don't stick to one color if you don't want to; team pinks with purples, oranges with yellow, pastel blues and greens, or go for a complete color clash. Doris

Right: Short veils were popular in the 1950s. This design, featuring polka-dot tulle and a bow, epitomizes the essence of 50s fun.

Below: Have fun with your petticoats! Work a classic single color, or layer up a few petticoats in varying shades to suit your design scheme.

Opposite: A rainbow of petticoats by Doris Designs.

Designs (www.dorisdesigns.co.uk) creates the most beautiful high-quality petticoats, each made of over thirty-six meters of double-layered, soft, light chiffon, which gives them wonderful body and bounce.

Veils varied in length during the 50s, but an iconic look that characterizes the period is the short and pouffy veil that sat on top of the head. These veils tended to be hip- or elbow-length, some as short as neck-length. Shorter veils look super cute with a ballerina-style gown. Saucer hats with veils attached were also popular. Vintage wedding dress suppliers will be able to recommend a great veil look.

Above: Pillbox hats and veils were hugely popular in the 1950s. This design is by Candy Anthony.

Right: A pretty pastel 50s-inspired headpiece by the Couture Company.

Opposite: Glamorous 1950s-inspired diamanté accessories.

A chic and elegant choice is the birdcage veil. Many designers crafting headpieces have variations of the birdcage veil in stock, but it's easy to make your own. The netting itself can be easily purchased from your local fabrics store and attached to a pretty brooch or decorative comb in your hair. There are many easy-to-follow birdcage veil tutorials online.

Keep accessories simple; a pretty beaded clutch bag, pearl earrings, or a choker-style necklace featuring various original vintage elements. Little white gloves will add a beautiful, chic finishing touch to a 50s-inspired wedding day wardrobe. Cornelia James (www.corneliajames.com) offers the very best selection of fashion and bridal gloves online, but also take a look at BHLDN (www.bhldn.com).

To retain an authentic look, opt for a pair of mid- to high-heel stiletto shoes. Many shoe designers offer this style in their collections and they can be purchased easily from department stores, but, in the spirit of the playful era, consider designing your own shoes! Milk & Honey Shoes (www.milkandhoneyshoes.com) offer superb and simple online design services, where you can tailor every single aspect of your shoe design. Match a leopard print open-toe heel with layers of red petticoats under a 50s vintage dress for some super fun wow factor. Brides who don't enjoy wearing heels can still look great in ballet-style flats with a 50s gown.

THE 1950S BRIDE

Tahuonia wears an original 1950s full-circle
tulle wedding dress, restored by Elizabeth Avey.
A sweetheart neckline can be more flattering than
a straight neckline and also softer on the face.
The soft net layer on top of all the other layers
lends a girly, playful style to the outfit.

Here, an original 50s lace wedding dress, restored by Fur Coat No Knickers, shows a little bit of leg but covers up the neckline. Cotton lace and high necklines were very typical of late 1950s bridal fashion. The lace is soft and flattering. You can lift the dress with layers of petticoats or keep it more natural and go without.

BEAUTY

Beauty companies had a field day in the 1950s; their target market was the women encouraged to stay at home and become homemakers. Following the scarcity of products during the war, every woman now wanted a full set of make-up and most women would apply a full face of makeup before starting their day. A woman was expected to look well-groomed at all times: 1950s makeup guides instructed a woman to check herself regularly throughout the day to make sure she looked good from top to toe! Because of this, a bride didn't look much different in terms of her hair and make-up than she would on a regular day.

Hairstyles were influenced by Hollywood's leading ladies– think Monroe, Hepburn, Bardot, and Kelly. Modern-day hairstyles that echo those of the 50s include the classic chignon, or bun, or softly set curls and a neatly-coiffed updo. Volume can be added to longer hair with a subtle bouffant.

Ladies with short hair can pull off a classic Audrey Hepburn look, and brides who would rather wear their locks loose can look to Marilyn Monroe for inspiration by adding a voluminous wave.

Top Tip

A matte red lipstick will require much less reapplication than a glossy lipstick.

Brides looking for a more rock 'n' roll or rockabilly 50s style might want to play with a more adventurous hair style, such as a pompadour bangs set high, usually with the rest of the hair dragged back into a neat ponytail.

A typical makeup look of the 50s could be described as "girl next door meets pinup"; it was fresh-faced and pretty with glowing skin and sultry, sexy, doe eyes—the 50s bombshell! Eyebrows were neatly defined but thicker than in previous decades, some with a square end that tapered into a neat but more defined arch (see Audrey Hepburn). Invest in a good brow pencil to practise your best 50s arch or have your brows professionally shaped before your wedding.

Red lipstick worn with red nails was hugely popular in the 50s—a style statement that is just as glamorous today. Lips were overdrawn with a liner to make them appear bigger (Monroe used this technique). But pastel colors also ruled in this decade, and pink led the way. Audrey Hepburn is quoted as having said that she "believed in pink!" Experiment with shades of pink lipstick or go for a simple gloss and focus more on the eyes—just remember to keep it subtle and elegant.

Eyeshadow should be kept fairly simple—light browns and neutral shades. The key component for eyes was eyeliner. A wing applied using a liner pencil adds instant glamour, with a hint of pinup/screen-siren sex appeal.

DÉCOR AND DETAILS

The 50s was such a playful era; there is lots of inspiration on which to draw to give your wedding reception a wonderful retro feel. Go for full-on cinematic glamour, making reference to the movies stars of the day. Create a pastel color explosion with pretty cupcakes, stationery, table décor, and balloons, or go for a full-on rock 'n' roll-style party.

There are some very talented cake designers out there who love to experiment with new assignments and create sensational sugary masterpieces. Have fun with your cake design, or go for an original vintage 50s cake topper—you can buy them online (try the site www.fancyflours.com). A mass of pretty little cupcakes decorated to suit your color scheme is also fun.

The 1950s is a great era for color inspiration. Pastel shades were hugely popular. An easy and super fun way to incorporate a rainbow of color at your wedding is to hang paper pom-poms. Ready-made pom-poms are readily available online—order a variety of colors and hang them at different heights.

Vintage paraphernalia that can be used to create a styled scene can be found in most thrift shops. Look to 50s prom culture for inspiration. One of the most fun weddings I ever attended was modeled after the Enchantment Under the Sea Dance from the movie *Back to the Future*! Ask your stationer to design some 50s-style prom party invites. Set the stage with a backdrop of foiled tinsel strips, play rock 'n' roll, and ask your guests to dress the part. Set up a photobooth and provide props for your guests to have fun with—put out cat's-eye sunglasses for the ladies and little pots of Brylcreem for the gents. Serve 50s diner-style French fries and consider asking an event stylist to design a dessert table that incorporates miniature milkshakes, along with striped straws, cookies, cakes, and ice cream.

HERE ARE SOME CULTURAL REFERENCES TO INSPIRE YOU:

- Movies: *Gentlemen Prefer Blondes*, *Funny Face*, and even more modern productions such as *Back to the Future* and *Grease*
- The Oscars and Hollywood red carpet style
- Movie stars: Marilyn Monroe, Elizabeth Taylor, Grace Kelly, Audrey Hepburn, Sophia Loren, Brigitte Bardot, Jayne Mansfield
- Music: bebop, doo-wop, rock 'n' roll, Buddy Holly, Elvis Presley, Little Richard
- Pastel colors
- Jukeboxes
- Fifties diners, milkshakes, and fries

Left and below: Pretty pastel sweet treats. This birdcage wedding cake was designed by Amanda Baird, of the Utterly Sexy Café.

107

Above: Laser-cut stationery in pretty pastel pinks and blues and featuring a 50s-inspired pink flamingo, designed by Cutture.

Left: Serve miniature milkshakes and fries to evoke a 50s diner atmosphere.

Alternatively, look to the cinema for inspiration; Hollywood is full of style references. Host an Oscars-style party with a black-tie dress code. Hire a red carpet for some tongue-in-cheek humor and get a speciality props company to create some light-up signs in your initials. Look for cinemas that can be hired as venues, or project a 50s movie onto one of your venue walls; you don't even need the sound on, the movie itself will help to emphasize the vibe. Serve popcorn in cartons.

Hire a crooner who can entertain your guests with classics by the likes of Frank Sinatra, or embrace your inner Elvis and go all out with the rock 'n' roll party style. Hire a band to play bebop and jive—have some silly fun and try a *Grease*-style dance-off. Look for companies who specialize in jukebox rentals. For some truly sensational and glamorous entertainment, consider hiring a 50s style burlesque troupe.

For authentic transportation, an old-fashioned Buick, pink Cadillac, or Chevrolet is what's needed. Go online to find your nearest vehicle-renting service.

Above: Create a high school prom scene and style a dessert table with milkshakes, cookies, and all kinds of sweet treats. A caterer and stylist will be able to create a dessert table that's as sweet to look at as it is to taste.

REAL BRIDE

MADELEINE & GEOFFREY'S WEDDING
MAY 4, 2012

Dress Replica 1950s dress and veil by Joanne Fleming Design (www.joanneflemingdesign.blogspot.com).

Accessories I ensured that my accessories all fitted with the 1950s style. My veil was embroidered with vintage lace from a nightgown of my mother's. My hairpiece was made by my friend and amazing artist Emma Houlston. In the interest of authenticity my fur shrug was genuine vintage and belonged to the grandmother of a friend. The shoes were Rachel Simpson (www.rachelsimpsonshoes.co.uk).

What inspired you to wear a beautiful 1950s-style lace wedding dress? I always wanted a vintage-style dress and the 50s cut best suited my figure, in addition to being perfect for dancing! I also felt that as a relatively young bride, the shorter length was fun and didn't make me look like I was dressing up in my grandma's clothes. I loved how it nipped me in at the waist with the layers and layers of skirt swirling around, each one edged with the palest pink silk. The lace was beautiful, elegant and set the tone for the rest of the wedding—it was present in the décor too.

What do you love most about the dress? The sleeves were a must for me, but I loved the elegance they brought to the dress, especially in such beautiful lace.

Décor and details I collected vintage linen tablecloths and napkins. I didn't want to imitate a vintage feel; I wanted it to be authentic. The flowers were grouped in vintage vases of differing heights and sizes; the cakes were presented on vintage cake stands. For the table settings I stamped luggage tags with navy lettering and tied them to the napkins with lace ribbons. Every table was just a little bit different; we had long trestle tables and the combination of the embroidered cloths, the place settings, the cluster of vintage vases, and soft seasonal flowers evoked a simple and elegant English vintage tea party vibe without being too country fair. The large paper fans and globes were sourced online.

Advice for other brides who are looking to recreate this kind of look? Combine carefully sourced genuine vintage pieces—be it clothes, accessories, or décor—with clever modern copies, and find ways to hand-make items, too. Also, keep it simple—less is definitely more.

REAL BRIDE

BARBARA & MARK'S WEDDING
APRIL 30, 2011

Dress Bespoke by Candy Anthony, London.

Shoes Picked them up in a little shop in Basel.

Accessories I purchased my headpiece online at www.talulahblue.folksy.com. My sister made the knitted bow that I wore after the church. Vintage gloves from my sister-in-law.

What inspired you to wear a beautiful 1950s-style wedding dress? I've always loved 1950s-style dresses, so I wanted that for me. I didn't stick to one era; I loved the idea of 1960s dresses and makeup for my bridesmaids—they have the legs and faces for it! I bought the yellow polka-dot fabric, and they were made by my friend's mom.

What do you love most about the dress? Along with the way the dress nips you in at the waist, my favorite bit is probably the polka-dot overlay. It adds a little bit of funk to a beautiful, classic 50s dress. When I tried it on, I knew it was the one immediately.

Do you have any advice for other brides who are looking to recreate this kind of look? Give yourself enough time to really get the right pieces. I bought a couple of different styles of gloves before my sister-in-law arrived from Australia, days before the wedding, with a pair that were exactly right. Also, look online; there are such fantastic vintage finds on there and at a fraction of the price of things being sold at wedding fairs. And, finally, don't underestimate the talents of your friends and family. My sister did a lot of the menus and other designs, as well as create my bow on the day. And my mom's friend made my bridesmaids' dresses. It means being able to have everything exactly as you want it, without having to spend ridiculous amounts.

The 1960s

The 60s saw a new sense of optimism. An artistic and cultural revolution was taking place; new music, fashion, and art burst onto the scene. The trendsetters were the young and the free-spirited–they were the "youthquake" (baby boomers born after World War II who had grown up with a different attitude). Mod culture was established, with slick made-to-measure suits and vespas for the boys, and tiny miniskirts, huge beehives, and fake lashes for the girls. Mod poster girls included the likes of supermodels Twiggy and Jean Shrimpton.

On the political scene, nuclear war didn't happen but the Vietnam War did, inspiring a generation to seek peace and spirituality: the hippy movement was born. Women renewed their sense of political activism and embraced a new modern look; hemlines sat at thigh length and A-line dresses freed them from the constraints of a corset.

John F. Kennedy's election to President of the United States in 1961 was to play catalyst to a huge shift in fashion trends. His wife, Jacqueline, became a fashion icon. Known for her impeccable grooming and chic sense of style, she has been copied by women all over the world, including brides. Other famous weddings that captured the bridal fashions of the time included Elizabeth Taylor and Richard Burton in 1964, Frank Sinatra and Mia Farrow in 1966, and Elvis Presley and Priscilla Beaulieu in 1967.

In the United States, bridal fashion continued to take inspiration from the Parisian fashion houses of Givenchy and Balenciaga, but the world's fashion gaze was firmly shifting to the Kings Road and Carnaby Street in London, where young trendsetters fresh out of design school were taking the scene by storm. They included the "High Priestess of Sixties Fashion," Mary Quant, credited for creating the miniskirt, and Biba, founded by Barbara Hulanicki, whose signature looks included long, bias-cut dresses in deco-style prints. These designers went on to influence bridalwear across the globe throughout the 60s.

Dress style best suited to:
petite, slender figures, and long legs.

Key bridal looks of the period:
- Mini, midi (ankle-skimming), and maxi dresses
- Long slender skirts—a slim silhouette
- A-line dresses
- Empire waistlines
- Knee boots and flat white shoes
- White tights
- Beehives, bouffants, and bangs
- The classic Audrey-style chignon
- Peter Pan collars
- Smock tops
- Hippie-style kaftans
- Puff sleeves or sleeveless
- Daisy motifs

VINTAGE INSPIRATION

Below: A trendy couple and their wedding party stand in front of the Little Church Around the Corner after their Manhattan wedding in 1966. The groom, Terence Burns, wears a velvet tuxedo, while the bride, Jacqueline Collins, and her bridesmaids wear lace minidresses.

Above: Siji and Cosiba Osunkoya, Nigeria, 1962. Cosiba wore an empire-line gown with an A-line skirt in a heavy cream silk brocade. It had a boat neckline in front with a low plunge neckline behind.

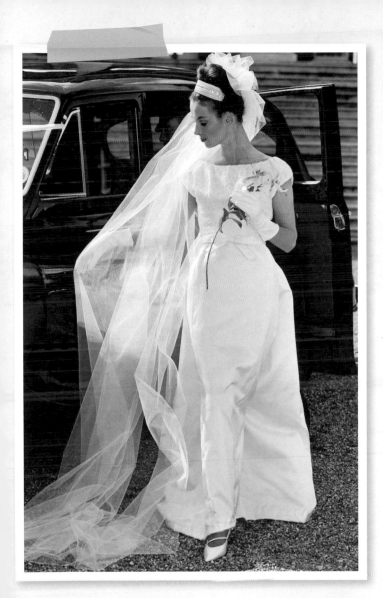

Above: A classic John French bridal image from 1961.

Top right: Corinne, pictured here with her father, on her wedding to Frank in June 1965. The wedding dress was second hand and was sold again after she wore it.

Right: Paul and Shirley Fleming, 1962. Shirley's bateau-neck dress cost about $18.

FASHION

The first part of the decade saw very little change in bridal fashion. The style of wedding dress made popular by Grace Kelly in the 50s (tight bodices and tulip skirts) continued to be popular, but the huge shifts in everyday fashion that emerged in the early 1960s soon filtered through to bridalwear. Contrary to popular belief, 60s bridal fashion wasn't all about the minidress. While the minidress made an impact from about halfway through the decade in bridalwear, the full-length, narrow A-Line and the empire-line silhouettes were the staples of the wedding day wardrobe throughout much of the 60s.

The empire line flatters most body shapes and is a fabulous design for those with a smaller bust or a more pear-shaped body; it will flatter you in all the best places and you won't need any support underwear either! Empire-line wedding dresses can be short or long to suit your preference.

Some of the shorter empire-line dresses in the 60s morphed into a more baby-doll look, mimicking a loose-fitting negligée or short, sleeveless dress suggestive of something a young child might wear. This look was intentional and mirrored the style of fashion made popular by the likes of supermodels Twiggy and Jean Shrimpton.

Right: This knee-length wedding dress is a replica vintage style, created for this bride who loves the mod style, by Glory Days Vintage.

Opposite: This short wedding dress design by Candy Anthony features an empire line and bow—both typical design features seen on many 60s wedding dresses.

Simple thigh-length shift dresses certainly had their day in the 60s and perfectly suited the new mod subculture that was emerging. Dresses tended to be sleeveless and minimalist in terms of embellishment; you are more likely to see a dress sporting a daisy motif than encrusted with Swarovski crystals and other sparkly embellishment. Another key feature for the 60s look was bows—often incorporated to draw attention to a particular design aspect of the dress.

Reflective of the age that introduced us to "flower power" and the hippy movement, daisies became hugely popular in the 60s. The daisy is said to represent innocence, purity, and love. It was seen as lace motifs on wedding dresses, as floral trim on hats and headpieces, and in bridal bouquets. You can use the daisy motif in a modern wedding look through accessories such as a headpiece or clutch bag. Customize a simple shift dress by adding a daisy trim and wrap the same trim around your bouquet. You could also have simple bandeaux made for your bridesmaids using the same trim, for a coordinated look.

Traditional dress trains fell out of favor during the 60s—more popular was the Watteau train, which fell from the shoulder blades to the hemline of the gown.

Dresses would often be worn with a full-length wedding coat. These were helpful for covering shoulders at a time when it was still unacceptable to bare them in church. Opera-length gloves would be worn over bare arms. Huge romantic cinema hits like *Dr. Zhivago* inspired the use of fur or faux fur on coats and even some dresses, often featured fur trim. You can still purchase maxi coats online and via speciality suppliers, but a dressmaker should also be able to replicate one. Take a look at pop singer Lulu's wedding day ensemble for her marriage to Bee Gees singer Maurice Gibb—she wore a full-length, fur-trimmed hooded coat with her dress.

Above: This bride, who lives a mod lifestyle and wanted to reflect this on her wedding day, found her original 1960s wedding dress in a thrift shop.

Another popular cover-up was the cape. The 60s bridal cape has been reinterpreted by several modern-day designers—take a look at the stunning duchesse lace cape on BHLDN (www.bhldn.com) or an exquisite 1960s vintage, open-back, full-length bridal cape with train, designed by London's Circa Vintage Brides (www.circabrides.com).

Various shoe styles were worn by brides, but they tended to be mostly white in color and featured a low heel. A pair of white patent go go boots with a square heel would have adorned the legs of a more fashion-conscious bride. Simple pumps with a kitten heel or a more chunky Cuban heel were popular too, perhaps featuring a decorative buckle or bow. Scour the web to find pretty shoe clips to add to a pair of plain pumps of your own.

The traditional wedding veil became less popular during the 60s as the short, angular new haircuts—made fashionable by Vidal Sassoon—didn't really suit a traditional long veil look. They were replaced by very short, pouffy veils, similar to those seen in the 50s but even shorter and more "fly away" in style, or by "fingertip" veils, which fell to the length of the ends of the fingers. These were often adhered to a saucer hat or pillbox headpiece. Some brides also wore chiffon or silk headscarves in place of a veil. The floppy hat also became an iconic look of the 60s, particularly seen from the mid-decade onwards.

As the decade drew to a close, the war in Vietnam prompted a tidal wave of young people to turn their attention to

Above: A champagne-colored original 1960s mod-style minidress with pearl beading, from Unforgettable Vintage Brides.

them featuring a pointed tip over the back of the hand. If you are interested in designer bridalwear, look out for labels such as Belville Sassoon, famous in the 60s and 70s for their eveningwear creations and for dressing high society brides, and Emma Domb, whose gowns created in the 50s and 60s have become much sought-after designs. For a brilliant modern-day interpretation of 60s fashion, look at bridalwear designer Tobi Hannah and her "youthquake" collection (www.tobihannahbridal.co.uk).

Wedding bouquets in the sixties tended to be quite small—tight posies or dainty spray bouquets were common. To pull off a more relaxed bohemian look, ask your florist to incorporate lots of fresh wild-looking foliage and create a "just-picked" look. Blooms that define the era well include daisies, sunflowers, echinacea, and gerbera; go for something simple like a plain daisy bouquet or mix a whole bunch of color together into something more bright and eclectic (inspired by Andy Warhol's pop art colorings).

spiritualism, peace, and love, and the hippie movement was born. This translated beautifully into bridalwear with its signature loose, long maxi dresses and midi dresses that skimmed the ankle—kaftan-style gowns made of floaty chiffon fabrics. Dress designs would take inspiration from the Far East, and hippie-style dresses were produced largely in lightweight cotton fabric. The barefoot, bohemian bride with her carefree approach to style took steps into the early 70s, where this book focuses on the look in more detail.

Original 60s wedding dresses are available via most speciality vintage wedding dress suppliers; undertake a search online for a 60s wedding gown, and you are likely to find both mini- and maxi-style dresses that feature an empire-line bodice, decorative bows, daisy motifs, possibly a detachable train, fabrics of brocade, silk, chiffon, guipure lace, sleeves that are capped and three-quarter or full-length—some of

Above left: These colorful shoes are crafted from vintage kimonos by designer Hetty Rose and would make a beautiful addition to any wedding-day wardrobe.

Opposite: An original 1960s vintage lace wedding dress from Elizabeth Avey.

THE 1960S BRIDE

Gia wears the "Lizzie" dress by Circa Vintage Brides. The "baby doll" dress is so accurate to the times–very Biba/Twiggy. This modern take on a 60s-style gown has a flowing train that gives it a bridal twist. Never forget that people see the bride from behind as much as they do from the front at a wedding.

Gia wears a simple, classic, Audrey Hepburn-esque 1960s tulip dress with beaded neckline detail. It is an original vintage dress by Heavenly Vintage Brides. This style of gown is a beautiful option for those looking for something truly elegant and demure for their wedding day.

BEAUTY

When it comes to hairstyles, the 60s is an era pretty much defined by the beehive. Although the beehive originated in America in the 50s, it wasn't until the following decade that it became hugely popular, thanks largely to influential stars of the time such as Brigitte Bardot and the pop group the Ronettes. This hairstyle provides instant glamour and volume and tends to suit most people. It comes in various guises, some of which suit more flyaway hair, and can be worn both low and subtle or with higher impact (Bardot wore her beehive in a more loose, tousled look, for instance). Speak to a professional stylist about which particular style will suit you best and try the look before your wedding.

A classic chignon, made famous by Audrey Hepburn in her 1961 movie *Breakfast at Tiffany's*, is a more relaxed style that would suit brides seeking an elegant look on their wedding day. The chignon is one of my favorite styles for a bride. I love the way stylists today create a slightly more modern "messy" version of this look that still retains elegance.

Another hairstyle that typifies the elegant and glamorous 60s is the bouffant, and while this style might not be as popular today, a modern interpretation styled by a professional can create a really chic look for those who wish to make their hair look more voluminous. Once again, experiment with this style during a hair trial.

It is no surprise, then, that by the mid-1960s, the number one hair product was hairspray! If you prefer a more natural, loose style, look to the bohemian, hippie styles that came into fashion towards the end of the decade. Wear a single flower in your hair or go for more of a statement with a floral circlet or a daisy chain headpiece. Alternatively, work the "flip" look, where shoulder-length hair is flipped outwards at the end—this simple and elegant hairstyle works beautifully with an Alice headband.

Short hair was catered to in the 60s by master hairstylist Vidal Sassoon. He created a trend for very short, sharply-cut hair for both women and men, which is still enjoyed by many today. Twiggy's short, slick, pixie-cut locks were also copied by women in droves, as was her perfect, pale complexion, with just a touch of pink blush. This childlike look of innocence was a key look of the time.

Typical 60s makeup is defined by a very pale lip and huge eyes, with dramatic, thick lashes and winged eyeliner (see Hepburn in *Breakfast at Tiffany's*). Hepburn's eyes were kitten-like with their huge fluttery, feathery lashes and thick black winged eyeshadow. Her brows were still thick, but much softer and less black, and her lips were pale pink and glossy. Stick to pale pinks, nude, and peach shades for your lip.

It was all about the eyes in the 60s. Blacks, whites, grays, and blues were used as eyeshadow. Take a look at Elizabeth Taylor's eyes in the 1963 movie *Cleopatra*; her exotic styling in this film had a huge influence on both fashion and beauty styles during the decade. Both Twiggy and "It girl" Edie Sedgwick wore huge false lashes on top and sported a set of painted lower lashes. This look beautifully epitomized the mod look of the era. Experiment with false lashes if you have not used them before to help you recreate that authentic, sexy, doe-eyed look on your wedding day. Take a pack of spare false lashes along on the day, just in case!

DÉCOR AND DETAILS

If you love the idea of the "swinging sixties," you have a perfect excuse for styling your wedding using a pop art explosion of fun color, but remember to keep it stylish and avoid being too gimmicky to prevent your guests from thinking they're attending a theme party!

A great start is to scour the websites dedicated to people who live a mod lifestyle; you'll find some fantastic sites online that are full of style inspiration.

Many prop companies will rent out furniture that can help evoke a sense of the 60s; use perspex chairs (look for companies who rent out pod seats, tulip chairs, or Panton chairs) and panels decorated with 60s icons or 60s-inspired artwork or floral patterns, to divide rooms into intimate seating booth areas for your guests. Alternatively, if you're looking for styling that takes more of a crunchy influence—more "flower power"—then consider creating seating areas with rustic appeal. If your wedding is being held outdoors, layer rugs on the ground for people to sit on: you can purchase inexpensive, brightly colored rugs from places like Ikea. Serve drinks in brightly colored wine glasses. If budget is a constraint, buy plastic glasses—the 60s was an era known for its plastic inventions, after all!

Recycle soup and bean cans and then decorate them with personalized Campbell's Soup-inspired art (your stationer should be able to do this for you) and use them as flower vases; fill them to the brim with daisies, sunflowers, and echinacea. You can easily re-create this scene indoors. Candle votives of all kinds of colors can be spread around your tables and filled with tealights. Also scatter real flower heads on tables and around table legs.

HERE ARE SOME CULTURAL REFERENCES TO INSPIRE YOU:

- Audrey Hepburn in *Breakfast at Tiffany's*
- Betty Draper in *Mad Men*
- Famous style icons: Twiggy, Brigitte Bardot, Catherine Deneuve, Anita Pallenberg
- Music: The Beatles, The Rolling Stones, Dusty Springfield, Aretha Franklin, The Supremes, The Beach Boys, Bob Dylan
- Film: *The Avengers*, *The Saint*, *Star Trek*, *Lost in Space*, Elizabeth Taylor in *Cleopatra*
- The beehive and the bouffant hairstyle
- Andy Warhol/pop art
- Geometric haircuts
- Flower power/hippie style
- Biba and Mary Quant
- Mods and rockers

MARGO

ANNABEL

JARED

ANNABEL AND PHIL

MENU

MENU

STARTER
SEVERN & WYE SMOKED SALMON
CAVIAR, CRÈME FRAICHE, CHIVES
CAPERS, RYE BREAD

MAIN
FILLET STEAK AU POIVRE
XO ARMAGNAC SAUCE, PEPPERCORNS
FINE GREEN BEANS

PUDDING
PIÈCE MONTÉE
PROFITEROLES, VANILLA ICE CREAM

COFFEE
CHOCOLATE TRUFFLES

SAUVIGNON, GAILLAC
MERLOT, LANGUEDOC

Rummage through thrift shops for 60s memorabilia to dress your venue—vases, Blenko glass pieces, lava lamps, floral fabrics, comics, vinyl records, and kitsch retro ornaments. There were some wonderful floral print designs that came out of the 60s (the Unikko poppy print by Marimekko is one of the most famous) that would make great table coverings or fabric backdrops to help you style a card/gift or cake table. Vintage *Vogue* magazines from the 60s can be purchased on eBay; they are not cheap but are really beautiful and fascinating pieces of history full of design and style inspiration from the era.

Above: A selection of floral 60s-style wedding stationery, created to match the wedding cake on page 131, by designers Emily and Jo.

Opposite: Use recycled tin cans and ask your stationer to create wrap-around labels like these ones by Emily and Jo, inspired by Warhol's soup cans. Use them as vases or table centerpieces.

Invest in some Warhol prints or 60s movie posters and frame them around your venue. See if you can rent a Vespa—your guests will love using it as a photo prop!

Set up a desk, *Mad Men*-style, with a kitsch 60s secretarial typewriter; you can purchase these on eBay in some lovely colors. Put out a secretarial-style "in tray" for your wedding cards, and get a hold of an old filing cabinet and fill it with old photographs of you and your friends and family for guests to enjoy looking through. You could also fill it with flowers or sweet treats!

Polaroid cameras were popular in the 60s. You can have amazing fun with modern instant cameras, which can be rented through speciality companies or purchased from Amazon. The film is quite expensive (it usually comes in packs of ten. ALWAYS buy multipacks online, it's much cheaper) but it's worth investing in on your wedding day as the instant images will create hours of fun for your guests.

Colorwise, you can either keep it relatively natural, with a palette of greens, oranges, yellows, and even golds, or focus on more psychedelic shades—fuchsia pinks, bright oranges and blues, purples and reds, even metallic accents. If the idea of too much color makes you dizzy, keep things simple with a stylish black and white monochrome palette.

When it comes to your wedding cake and stationery, try to keep your choice consistent with other design and styling aspects; so, if you've gone for a more bright and colorful floral style, stick to this for paper products and cakes also. I have seen some exquisite cakes covered in iced daisies, sunflowers, and echinacea. Retro sweets are always a treat with guests of any age; use the web to find a reputable retro sweets supplier where you can buy in bulk.

Musically it's easy to recreate a 60s party atmosphere. The soundtrack of the decade offers the Beatles, the Rolling Stones, Jimi Hendrix, Crosby, Stills, Nash & Young, Janis Joplin, the Who, Joe Cocker, the Grateful Dead. There are many bands that model themselves after the big pop groups of the time: hire one, or select your own playlist in iTunes to play a range of 60s tracks. She loves you, yeah, yeah, yeah!

For transportation, look at a VW camper van or keep it classic with a vintage 60s Daimler. You could even make a stylish "just married" exit in a Mini Cooper—*The Italian Job*-style!

LYNDA & DAMON'S WEDDING
FEBRUARY 11, 2012

Dress Dragonfly Dress Design
(www.dragonflydressdesign.co.uk).

Veil Vintage-inspired large pearl encrusted cap with veil by Sasso,
via Melle Cloche (www.mellecloche.com).

Accessories Vintage 1960s sparkly gold handbag; vintage fur stole; bangles and bracelets were
a mixture of vintage and department store finds.

Shoes Department store.

What inspired you to wear a beautiful 1960s-style lace wedding dress? I've always been
inspired by the fashion of the 1960s, and was instinctively drawn towards a style of dress from
this era. I love the simplicity and clean lines of the dress, as well as the cheeky and unusual peach
underlay. Once I had picked my dress, I decided early on that cutting my hair into a Mary Quant
bob was the way to go for me. I like the sleek and geometric style of the cut.

Do you have any advice for other brides who are looking to recreate this kind of look? I found
visual inspiration from a number of places, such as Pinterest.com, as well as looking at pictures of
icons from the 1960s. By incorporating various small 1960s-inspired elements into your day, you'll
quickly find that your day has that real vintage feel. This could include how you do your makeup
and even what music you play.

JESSICA & PAUL'S WEDDING
DECEMBER 23, 2010

Dress I made my dress using one of my mom's Simplicity patterns; she used to make many of her clothes during the 60s and I'm lucky that she kept her old patterns. The pattern was for a sleeveless dress with a full skirt and soft pleats. I made it from a pale ivory duchesse satin fabric and chose to add an organza layer over the skirt of the dress, which I edged with ivory ribbon. I chose an ivory and black theme for the wedding, and thus added a belt made from both black velvet and black satin ribbon. The belt emphasized the waist of the dress and added extra interest to the back, as it featured a large bow. I also found a 1963 pattern for a back-buttoned jacket that I thought would look perfect with my dress. I made the jacket from the same material as the dress itself, and sewed a blue ribbon bow to the inside for my "something blue"! The dress was finished with a three-tier and four-layer net petticoat, edged with ivory satin.

Hair Accessories The veil was by Caroline Castigliano. I edged it myself with ivory ribbon. I also wanted to incorporate the bow from the belt of the dress and the bow on the shoes. I removed a black velvet ribbon bow from a headband, and glued it to a hair clip to place in my hair.

Accessories I chose accessories that would complement both the dress itself and the era. The beautiful vintage pearl necklace was from Fur Coat No Knickers (furcoatnoknickers.co.uk). The shoes were Sergio Boscaro black patent leather, with a small stiletto heel and square toe. To complete the look, I found a brilliant vintage Kelly handbag and lace-trimmed vintage gloves.

What inspired you to wear an early 60s-style dress? I love the fashion and look from this era—full skirts becoming shorter in length than in the 50s, bigger hair and more exaggerated makeup.

What do you love most about the dress? The fact that I made it myself (even though that was definitely not the easy option)! It felt like a real achievement, a true labor of love! It also allowed me to be creative by adding extras that I thought would enhance the look.

Advice for other brides Don't feel that everything has to be expensive or true vintage; there are wonderful items that can enhance your wedding look to be found in all sorts of places. Don't be afraid to be different and creative with your look.

The 1970s

Our journey through vintage bridal fashion ends in the 1970s—an era that brings to mind a vision of the bohemian bride looking relaxed in her floaty, maxi dress, loose hair decorated with a floral crown, marrying her love in an informal, outdoor summer wedding ceremony. But it wasn't all about the barefoot bride; the 70s brought with it an explosion of new pop, punk, and glam rock music that had a big impact on fashion.

Bridalwear in the 1970s started out influenced by the flower-child hippy aesthetics of the late 60s and ended with a much slicker, almost masculine, disco-inspired look. In between, there was no predominant fashion that ruled the bridal runways; instead, the decade presented an eclectic and varied wedding day wardrobe, which included everything from the high-necked, billow-sleeved romantic look to kaftans, punk and fantasy-inspired design, Grecian-style dresses, and tailored trouser suits.

The hippie culture that began in the previous decade continued to enjoy popularity in the early 70s, but started to wane by the middle of the decade as a new hit on the musical scene was about to become the biggest musical genre since rock 'n' roll. On Valentine's Day 1970, David Mancuso opened his members-only club in New York City, and the disco scene was born. Disco enjoyed popularity throughout the whole of the 70s, peaking after the hit movie *Saturday Night Fever* was released in 1977. Disco had an instant influence on fashion and bridal fashion and, by the late 70s, brides were wearing draped lurex, Grecian dresses, and disco-style clothing.

Celebrity weddings that took place in the decade included Bianca and Mick Jagger in 1971, Princess Anne and Captain Mark Phillips in 1973, Elizabeth Taylor and Richard Burton in 1975, Don Johnson and Melanie Griffith in 1976, and Alana Hamilton and Rod Stewart in 1979.

Dress style best suited to:

a variety of figures, but looks best on taller girls.

Key bridal looks of the period:

- Barefoot, bohemian bride
- Grecian style/draped fabric
- Romantic medieval look
- Mob cap and milkmaid/prairie style/peasant dresses
- Maxi dresses
- Loose and flowing fabric
- Wide-brimmed floppy hats
- Tailored trouser/pant suits
- Puff shoulders and billowed "leg o' mutton" sleeves
- Punk, glam rock, and disco influences
- Loose, flowing hairstyles

VINTAGE INSPIRATION

Above: A John Bates 1970s dress design of pleated chiffon with a cape-style bodice echoing the elegant skirt, worn with a corsage belt and a veiled straw hat.

Above: Flamboyant wedding dress design by John Bates, circa 1975, with an exaggerated rever collar, art nouveau-style embroidered flowers on the skirt and ruched sleeves, and long, medieval-style cuffs. Worn with a matching veiled hat.

Opposite top: Welsh actress Nerys Hughes marries television cameraman Patrick Turley in London, 1972.

Right: Henrietta Countess Compton leaves Chelsea Registry Office with groom Peter Thompson and daughter Lara, 1974.

Above: Jacqueline Leatherby and David Shreeve, photographed on their beloved foldaway bikes, setting off on their honeymoon in 1978. Jacqueline wore a dress by Tallers and under-skirt and bodice by Marissa Martin. The fabulous boots were by the Chelsea Cobbler. Their daughter, Alice Shreeve, is one of the creative directors of the fashion label Belle & Bunty, who make vintage-inspired silk wedding dresses of their own.

FASHION

The 70s was a time when no particular bridal fashion led the way or dominated the era. Instead, the decade offered an eclectic mix of bridal fashion and several looks emerged; essentially, women chose to wear what they wanted and, fashion-wise, pretty much anything went. It was about being unique, individualistic, and having your own fashion identity. Yves Saint Laurent captured this spirit in his beautiful tailoring for women—a look typified by the likes of Bianca Jagger, who chose to wear a YSL tailored blazer, midiskirt, and floppy hat on her wedding to Mick Jagger in 1971.

Bridal designers were beginning to take inspiration from the past, acknowledging "retro" clothing as a source of style inspiration. The medieval and Victorian eras were particularly influential, hence the huge puff shoulders, long billowed sleeves, and medieval princess-style gowns that can often be seen from this era.

Full-length prairie or milkmaid-style dresses were also hugely popular. Evoking a peasant and gypsy aesthetic, many of these dresses featured a dust ruffle detail that circled the skirt hem and gave the wedding gown a very countrified look, in addition to high necks, ruffles, and huge Camelot sleeves.

The Grecian-style gown—a look made popular by Diane Von Furstenberg, who created draped jersey dresses—was another look to emerge in the 70s that is still hugely popular today.

While disco originated in the early part of the decade, it truly surfaced as a mainstream genre of music by 1975 and went on to have a big impact on bridal fashion. Bridalwear designers were focusing on much less structure in their designs and incorporating drapes, flowing capelets, batwings, and empire waists. They used stretchy polyester double-knit fabric, which draped beautifully, and oozed sex appeal. By the end of the decade, the demand for designer fashion had soared, influenced largely by the hip Studio 54 scene.

Nylon, polyester, and machine-made laces were readily available in the 70s, and these fabrics offered a more affordable alternative to silks, satins, and handmade laces. Wedding dresses were thus much more lightweight than they had been previously. They were also much more affordable, even though many still featured embellishment that made them look more expensive. Stretch polyester double knit was used widely towards the end of the decade, as was Dupont's "miracle fiber," Qiana.

Seventies bridal fashion is now enjoying a renaissance and appearing in some of the top bridalwear designers' latest collections. Contemporary designers who have taken inspiration from the 70s in their collections include Jenny Packham and Temperley London for their gorgeous Grecian-style gowns, and Allan Hannah, Circa Vintage Brides, and Stephanie Allin have all designed 70s-inspired trouser suits.

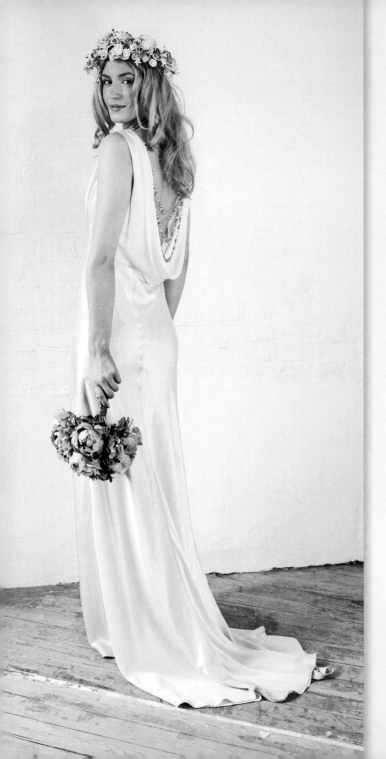

Halston was one of the most popular designers of the 70s, creating fluid jumpsuits, one-shoulder gowns, and flowing jerseys for the disco glitterati. Halston Heritage, the Halston diffusion line, released a collection of eight 70s-inspired wedding gowns in 2011 that ooze Studio 54 appeal.

Despite all the experimentation in design that took place in the 70s, the white wedding dress remained the first choice for most brides, and most mainstream wedding collections steered clear of the outrageous or gimmicky. The vast majority of brides sought tradition in their bridal style; the era saw a return of subtle candy colors, very pale pinks, blues and canary yellows, mob caps, blue ginghams, frills, and floppy hats.

Several fashion designers became successful during the 70s for both their bridal and evening wear. If you are keen to source an original vintage wedding dress from the 1970s, look out for designer labels by Halston, Christos, Jim Hjelm, Belville Sassoon, Priscilla of Boston, and John Burbridge. If you are interested in exploring specific designer labels, consult with a reputable vintage wedding gown specialist.

Left: The 70s looked to history for inspiration and took influences from the 1930s with maxi-length dresses, empire lines, and satin fabrics. You would be forgiven for thinking this dress was a 30s homage. The beaded back detail and the color of this design—by the State of Grace—give a real 70s hippy chic look to this dress.

Even gowns that were not designed to be bridalwear have become a popular choice of vintage wedding day attire Laura Ashley, for instance. Also check your local thrift shops and vintage concessions in department stores. Topshop has a fabulous vintage concession with Peekaboo Vintage (www.peekaboovintage.com), where clothes are usually grouped by color; they often stock some wonderful off-white/ivory day and evening dresses from the 70s that would make amazing wedding dresses.

Many twenty- and thirty-somethings planning their wedding today may have parents who were married in the 70s. Take a look through family photos to be inspired and get a vibe for the fashions of the time. My own mom chose a dark brown velvet minidress to wed my dad in late 1970. It featured dark orange circular patterns—about as unbridal as you could get. But, in the 70s, women chose to wear what they wanted and enjoyed experimenting with their own unique style.

The very best brand of shoes that has taken a strong influence from the platform styles of the 70s is Harriet Wilde. Harriet Wilde is stocked in Harrods and ships internationally via the Harriet Wilde website (www.harrietwilde.com). Designs feature platform heels and four-inch sling-back heels covered in disco-style glitter. They are incredibly comfortable, very well-produced shoes. Many modern brands run a line of wedge heels in their summer collections. Try Topshop (www.topshop.co.uk) or Kate Spade (www.katespade.com) for starters.

Above: Examples of original and 1970s-inspired bridal fashion, including a high-collared design by the State of Grace and, on the right, a find from Peekaboo Vintage.

Veils and headpieces in the 1970s were less poufed than they had been in the 60s, but were still generally long. The Juliet cap/cloche hat-style veil experienced some popularity again during this period and crescent headpieces were popular too—worn either directly on top of the head or towards the back with a veil usually attached. Many brides preferred to

Above: Floral crowns have seen a revival in recent times. Indicative of a relaxed, hippy-inspired look, they are perfect for the more bohemian bride. This design has been hand-crafted petal-by-petal using clay by accessories designer Lila. Opting for a replica piece instead of using real flowers means a precious heirloom can be created for future generations.

Right: Star headband design by Madeline Bride.

wear flower headpieces in their hair, floppy hats with trims, or bohemian-inspired floral crowns or circlets. Use Pinterest (www.pinterest.com) as a source of inspiration to find different flower crown designs and ask your florist to experiment. Alternatively, invest in a modern-day wax flower headpiece that will make a beautiful investment and inheritance piece. Up-and-coming label Lila produces the most exquisitely beautiful wax floral headpieces (www.lila-lila.com).

Seventies inspired cover-ups to keep you warm might include a beautiful tailored blazer. Pale blazers in white or ivory look so chic and very Studio 54, especially teamed with a Grecian-style dress. For the more bohemian-style bride, consider a shawl, which can be worn more casually. British designer Nicola Lokko of My Shell Me Shell (www.

my-shell-me-shell.com) specializes in producing exquisite vintage-inspired crocheted shawls that can be thrown over your shoulders to stay warm and can be worn again after the wedding day. Nicola's "ruffle shawl" from her Heirloom range features several layers of crochet that would make the perfect accessory for an outdoor summertime wedding. Alternatively, go for a Native American-inspired feather headpiece—use Etsy.com to source suppliers.

Above left: Chunky-heeled shoes, reminiscent of 70s styles, fashioned from original vintage pieces by designer Hetty Rose.

Above right: Raid your local thrift stores for original 70s paraphernalia and accessories.

THE 1970S BRIDE

If you want to take the 70s look to the max, take a chance on a pantsuit rather than a dress. This all-in-one bodice with wide leg trousers is still flattering, as it has the flare of a skirt but more movement. The silver adds both glamour and light-reflecting color that lifts the face. It is great to balance out the look with the short fur bolero for ultimate Hollywood hippy-glam style. Pantsuit and faux fur by the State of Grace.

The hippy, relaxed, natural influences of the 70s are really prevalant in this dress design by Katya Katya Shehurina. Fringing, a loose silhouette, and matte textures are all signature 70s looks. In both the 60s and the 70s, rebellion and antitradition came through in fashion and bridal design. This mask by designer Basia Zarzycka gives a nod to a veil without the full netting – it has all the mystery of a veil, with the embellishment and detail of a piece of jewelry. The look is finished with a colorful pair of chunky-heeled shoes by Hetty Rose.

BEAUTY

Things got very glossy in the 70s. Pearl essence was added to almost everything, so all the bold colors of the 1960s now became very shimmery and pastel in shade. The lips had extra gloss, giving a very wet sheen, and eyes would feature black mascara, black eyeliner, and shimmer eyeshadow, which would often match the color of the outfit being worn.

Women had more of a healthy glow in the 70s, as they began to play around with dewy foundations, fake tan, bronzing powders, and pearl essence on the cheekbones. This marked a significant change to beauty styles seen in the 60s and possibly marked a reaction against the pale, matte, two-tone face of that time. Women were also traveling more and a tan, from time spent in hotter climates, was very desirable.

Seventies makeup that best translates to a modern-day look includes healthy, glowing skin, natural lashes, and a simple lip gloss—think bohemian bride *au naturelle* and pick a bronzing powder that works with your complexion.

If you prefer to be more adventurous, ask a makeup artist to work on your eyes using subtle glitter-based shadows—think disco glam more than boho bride. And pack a couple of pairs of false lashes for any wedding day emergencies!

Hair began to get bigger again in the 70s and big, loose curls became very fashionable. Every decade has its classic updo and the 70s was no different; women would pile hair on top of the head to create the "top knot" style we are familiar with today. The front of the head would have a smooth finish as the hair was pulled tight, and shape and fullness was then created by twisting, backcombing, and pinning the hair on top of the head. Other classic styles that the 70s embraced were the bun and the chignon. Rather than scraping the hair tight, hair would be backcombed slightly and loosely shaped into a bun at the back of the head (either at the nape or slightly higher up), where it would be tightly pinned and pushed forward to give even more height and fullness, so that it wasn't flat against the head.

Perhaps one of the most famous hairstyles of the era, however, is the style modeled by *Charlie's Angels* TV star, Farah Fawcett. "The Farah," as it has come to be known, essentially involves a center parting, with big, soft, feathered waves: it's a great look for those with long hair. For shorter-haired brides, consider a loose pageboy-style bob. The look doesn't suit everyone, but it is regaining popularity for its retro appeal.

The 70s also embraced the natural afro in all its glory. So, either tame your tresses, or go as big as you like and add flowers to your look.

Opposite: For an original 70s-inspired look, keep makeup fresh faced, with glowing skin and lipgloss

Above: Experiment with colors around your eyes: blue and green eyeshadows were popular during this decade.

153

DÉCOR AND DETAILS

The 70s provides a wonderful range of retro inspiration for your wedding day, whether you are looking to set a relaxed bohemian scene, or a more glamorous disco-style environment. The trick to translating era style into a modern-day setting is to pick a few key pieces or aesthetics you enjoy rather than trying to replicate a whole look. Ditch any thoughts of a fancy dress party and focus on evoking a really elegant and chic, retro-inspired ambience.

If you are looking to re-create some Studio 54 cool, think decadent and luxurious jet-setting hedonists who enjoy sipping on cocktails in the finest bars while dancing to über cool 70s disco. Design your own cocktails for the day—this can be really fun (meet with your venue beforehand to discuss options and have an evening with your best friend choosing fun cocktail names). Use 70s movies, TV programs, disco tracks, and other references as table names, and consider draping staged areas with inexpensive fabric—silvers, golds, and metallics work beautifully with this cool, jet-set ambience.

Google "rent a disco ball" and, if your venue allows it, enhance your surroundings by renting specialty props and furniture—leather chaise longues and mirrors for instance. You can really have fun with this. Many companies create and rent out bespoke props, including giant retro-inspired letters that light up.

To really set the scene, consult with a specialty lighting service. Lighting hire is often overlooked as a wedding service, but can completely transform and enhance even the plainest of wedding venues.

A 70s disco, funk, and soul soundtrack will absolutely guarantee your guests filling the dance floor as the evening moves on. Think Gloria Gaynor, Donna Summer, Roy Ayres, Sister Sledge, Barry White, Marvin Gaye, K.C. and the Sunshine Band, and early Michael Jackson.

HERE ARE SOME CULTURAL REFERENCES TO INSPIRE YOU:

- Disco and glitter balls
- Studio 54
- Farah Fawcett and *Charlie's Angels*
- Movie hits: *Saturday Night Fever*, *The Godfather*, *Star Wars*, *Rocky*, *Jaws*
- John Travolta, Clint Eastwood, Robert Redford, Woody Allen, Al Pacino
- Music: disco, glam rock, punk, and soft rock
- Fashion: Diane Von Furstenburg, Vivienne Westwood, Fiorucci

When it comes to flowers, consider introducing plants as well as florals. Succulents make really beautiful table décor, and you can experiment with incorporating succulents into your wedding bouquet too. Look to hanging trailing plants from hanging planters. Burlap, which is readily available to purchase, can be used to wrap around glass jars of greenery.

If you are keen to incorporate flowers, consider a natural wildflower look, particularly if you are drawn to the boho/barefoot vibe, with white, neutral greens, and the odd splash of orange and yellow to add punches of color.

For a relaxed, bohemian-style wedding, consider working with a color scheme of greens, creams, and golds, and try to source some wicker furniture for romantic candle-lit seating areas. For the ultimate outdoor boho venue, consider renting a tent or yurt. A luxurious yurt, hand-crafted from sweet chestnut wood, covered in cream canvas would be perfect for a magical wedding under the stars. Yurts can be decorated inside with hanging décor, rugs, mats, beanbags, and even catered dining settings. Alternatively, cover hay bales with blankets and hang pretty lanterns.

Seventies memorabilia can be incorporated into your wedding day as tongue-in-cheek décor to make your guests smile, or as elegant pieces to really add to the ambience. It is entirely up to you how far you take the inspiration. Owl motifs were hugely popular at the time and Etsy is awash with cute retro-inspired owl designs. Also look to eBay for original 70s paraphernalia that can be used to style tables and seating areas—magazines, posters, fabric featuring 70s prints, and ornamental glasswear. Garage and yard sales are also full of such items.

A loose theme or matching aesthetic between your décor, stationery, and cake design will ensure a sense of consistency and make for some wonderful detail shots when it comes to your wedding photography. These elements of your wedding day provide the opportunity to be as traditional or creative as you want to be.

Wedding cakes can take on any form. For example, the cake featured on page 155 was designed to look like wicker to match the 70s wicker and rattan props. For something entirely different, opt for a cake covered in sparkle and edible glitter. Have a little fun with your catering too. Fondue sets were huge in the 70s—have a few set out so that your guests can dip marshmallows into chocolate or enjoy a savory treat instead, while reminiscing about childhood and the good old times. Consult with your venue or a catering company about how you can incorporate a little retro-inspired food fun into your wedding day.

Opposite: Beautiful wedding stationery by Berinmade, designed with cheeky 70s slogans and a neutral color palette to match the wicker and rattan elements used to style the fashion pages and also to tone with the wicker-inspired wedding cake design by Zoe Clarke Cakes on page 155.

Above: For 70s-inspired florals, focus on a more natural or wild flower look, and consider incorporating more greens and foliage into your bouquet.

REAL BRIDE

MARIA & NICK'S WEDDING
JUNE 25, 2011

Dress Mother-in-law's 1970s wedding dress.

Accessories All vintage jewelry. True to the era, I kept my hair simple with loose waves and parted down the center, and finished the look with a vintage crystal headband.

What inspired you to wear a beautiful original 1970s wedding dress? I have always been into vintage pieces, and dreamed of wearing a gorgeous vintage gown. I didn't think that I would be lucky enough to have a dress also worn by someone I love! It was actually the first wedding dress I ever tried on; when I saw it, I just knew it was the one. I couldn't believe that Nick's mom offered it to me, it felt like it was made for me. I kept it a secret from Nick and loved seeing his face when he realized that it was his mom's.

What do you love most about the dress? Well, the thing I love most is that it was worn thirty-two years ago by Nick's mom, Janette, and yes, his parents are still together! I am just in love with the beautiful sleeves–the lace top and the bell bottoms–they are perfection! Also, the only change to the dress (other than replacing the paper lining) was to open up the lace chest, as it was originally lined. I think it gave the dress more of a summer feel by allowing a little more skin to show through the lace. Lastly, the mix of textures the dress has–from lace, to very delicate flocked polka dots. Even though the dress was thirty-two years old, it still felt so fashion forward!

Details and décor We made use of baby's breath (*gypsophila*) for all of our bouquets and bouttonieres, which gave a 70s vintage look and feel.

Do you have any advice for other brides who are looking to recreate this kind of look on their wedding day? I think the most important thing is to find something that really suits you–who you are, what you love, and that you feel really beautiful in. There are no rules, and to mix old with new can be really fun and interesting. Plus, if you can find things to wear that are meaningful, it will make it all the more special.

Scent by Odette Toilette

Give a historic perfume a new lease on life on your wedding day by tracking down an original vintage scent just waiting to be opened up for a waft of history to come billowing out. Unless you want to spend a small fortune and play detective, many original scents are, alas, unavailable, but whenever possible I have suggested contemporary alternatives for a similar feel. Try also the Perfumed Court (www.theperfumedcourt.com), which sells decanted vintage bottles, making it affordable to buy by the milliliter. Luckily for us, many fragrance houses are raiding their archives and rereleasing former glories, so there are plenty of lovely fragrances to discover.

1920S

The fragrances of the Jazz Age are rather fond of novelty. Caron's Tabac Blond is a famous example, designed in tribute to the aroma of tobacco, and rather risqué for the time. Coty Chypre, a name which now refers to a whole genre of fragrance, technically dates to 1917, but truly belongs to the 20s. Named after Cyprus, birthplace of Venus, Coty Chypre is a bewitching, mossy forest in a bottle and, heartbreakingly, no longer available. It is irreplaceable, but it did influence Guerlain's Mitsouko, which adds fruit to the forest fragrance and is still available (www.guerlain.com). For that woodland feel, try also the contemporary Ormonde Woman by Ormonde Jayne (www.ormondejayne.com).

Nuit de Noël by Caron (www.parfumscaron.com) is another chypre, conjuring up the magic of Christmas. It is like a walk through pine trees, followed by a few glasses of eggnog. This scent gets a mention in Evelyn Waugh's novel *Vile Bodies*, and the wrap-around band on the original bottle was designed to resemble a flapper's headpiece (see picture opposite). Don't save it up for Christmas; it needs to be worn regularly. It is still available today from Les Senteurs (www.lessenteurs.com), or try Precious One by British perfumer Angela Flanders (www.angelaflanders-perfumer.com). She also sells an herbal anti-moth spray to keep your wedding dress free from holes.

Caron's Narcisse Noir is also earlier than the 20s, but was referenced by simply everyone in the decade, including Noel Coward. This is neroli with a woody kick, strangely oily while a little dusty. It is nicely intoxicating and especially suited to a silk dress. You can buy it today.

Royal Bain de Caron is like taking a bath in an absurdly extravagant Hollywood hotel suite. It was originally designed as a bath splash and can still be used as such, in addition to being used directly on the skin—think sherbet and Jean Harlow. It's still for sale in a gorgeous bottle (www.escentual.com). Prada Candy is similar but with a naughty undertone.

1930S

This is a decade of unusual and distinctive perfumes that beg to be worn with a bias-cut dress. Shocking by Schiaparelli really does smell like the fashion house's eponymous hot pink color. It is photographed here in "nips" form. Not as obscene as they sound, nips were one of many ingenious packaging formats of the time. In the United States one could purchase fine fragrance from vending machines, and nips were packs of individual applications, each housed in a tiny glass vial. You would go to the powder room of a restaurant, get your pack of nips, and snap the end of a vial off to apply. Cult British perfume house 4160 Tuesdays has developed a tribute to Shocking called Lights On, Lights Off, for those yearning for a bit of that luscious scent (www.4160Tuesdays.com). Ta'if by Ormonde Jayne (www.ormondejayne.com) also brings floral decadence, with rose mingled with dates and orange blossom. Warning: will make people swoon.

Further gutsiness comes from En Avion by Caron, a paeon to taking to the skies, made in honor of female pilot Amelia Earhart. In the thirties, flying was suitably luxurious to be an inspiration to perfumers. This is all leather, diesel, goggles and a glass of champagne. Guerlain also had an aviation-inspired scent, Vol De Nuit, which is still available. Wear on your honeymoon flight to feel as though you're going first class, even if in economy.

Fleurs de Rocaille by Caron is a restrained, elegant, almost abstract floral—not to be confused with their more recent Fleur de Rocaille. Pour un Homme is my token recommendation for the groom, and is only to be worn by very suave gentlemen. It brings such simplicity, focused on a pairing of lavender and vanilla, and smells divine. You could imagine Fred Astaire flying around a dance floor wearing this. Ginger would be in Fleurs de Rocaille.

1940S

The 1940s marked a gradual hand over of the power politics of perfume from France to America. It is remarkable that Rochas Femme made it to market, composed in a rickety building in Paris under Nazi occupation. Wear this with furs, as it is a fruity, deep plummy perfume with plenty of cumin these days. Caron's Pour Une Femme, housed in a whimsical bottle of a female bust, has a smell resembling battenberg cake–in the best possible way–and would be wonderful paired with a tea dress.

Robert Piguet's Bandit is altogether gutsier, composed by the intriguing, rock 'n' roll female perfumer Germaine Cellier. This is the antithesis of frou-frou and is not to be worn with a meringue of a dress. Think Lauren Bacall in *The Big Sleep*. As a comparatively more recent alternative, Lauder's Azurée has the same dry, herbal, leather aspect. It's also good to wear when strong-arming the in-laws.

Postwar brought cheer with English house Penhaligon's Eau de Verveine marrying a high citrus song with herbal clary sage (they recently raided their archives so you can buy this one today). It also brought the rapid rise of Christian Dior and his New Look, accompanied by the blockbuster Miss Dior, which (watch out) is today named Miss Dior Original, as a different scent took the Miss Dior name. This is a beautiful green chypre, classic and elegant.

A contemporary take on the 40s scent is Swiss perfumer Andy Tauer's Une Rose Chyprée (www.tauerperfumes.com), which is both dry and luscious, womanly and androgynous, and utterly unique.

1950S

Fifties perfumery continued the leather handbag vibe with Cabochard, by the elegant couture house run by Madame Grès; it is like a gentler version of 40s scent Bandit and savvy fragrance-lovers can pick it up online for a bargain. People will think you're wearing something expensive, but it really isn't.

Coming up alongside the suave, Bette Davis-style scents are a troop of girly pink florals, dripping in aldehydes—highly appropriate for the era of Hitchcock Blondes and Marilyn Monroe. Chantilly by Houbigant is indeed like fine lace, or that delicious, sinful cream. It is French patisserie in a bottle: raspberries, almonds, sponge cake, butter. First released in

the 1940s, it really hit its stride in the postwar housewife culture of 50s America. Chantilly is not at all the same these days, so try White Musk Libertine from The Body Shop for that whipped cream feel, or Editions de Parfum Frederic Malle and his Lipstick Rose for a pastiche of a beauty counter in a mall, with rose, raspberry, violets, and vetiver. For a softer shade of pink, the classic 50s scent Diorissimo by Dior is readily available, providing an incredible synthesis of lily of the valley and an almost swanlike elegance. All are glorious for weddings, especially with fuschia lipstick.

Youth Dew by Estée Lauder is a balsamic, resinous, treacley scent, originally released in 1953 as a bath oil, before converting over to perfume. It smells regally old fashioned, and would be perfect with the going-away outfit, as you rush through the crowd of guests and into the car with your fellow, leaving a mysterious puff of fragrance behind. Also pictured is Great Lady, a now disappeared perfume from another of the new breed of American beauty entrepreneurs of the time, Evelyn Westall.

Floris Rose Geranium bath oil is not technically 1950s, but Floris sent this to Marilyn Monroe, and it produces an incredible scented bath, plus the turquoisey peacock color is quite something. Use it for pre-wedding bathing in a rolltop bath; your skin will be highly perfumed afterwards.

1960S

This era moved towards light, fresh scents as a reaction to the more formal, cocktail dress perfumes of the past. This was the era of Eau Sauvage, the Steve McQueen of aftershaves, which created a sexy new smell of clean. Vivara by Pucci encapsulated the 60s if you were Brigitte Bardot. It is the Riviera in a bottle, and was composed to reflect Emilio Pucci's desire for women to smell of sand and sea. Similarly, the long-gone Eau Vive by Carven, garbed in signature green colors, is like a sports tonic, and might be sprayed in between sets of tennis on the lawn.

The minidress wearers among you might like the starkly futuristic and urban Calandre by Paco Rabanne, curiously named after the metal grille on the front of luxury cars. This is the fragrance version of *The Jetsons*, first released in 1969 and smelling like it came out last year (available online).

You may disagree, but, for the doe-eyed model on the box, the moment for wearing Tweed really was "now." Lenthéric, the house behind Bouquet Tweed, began as a milliner in the 18th century, until hairdressing-heir Guillame set up a perfume operation in the Belle Epoque period. "Bouquet" was Lenthéric's way of denoting a lighter, eau de toilette version of the original Tweed. This woody chypre fragrance is pulled together; it's quietly assertive and not at all girly. The readily available Calèche from Hermès is a nice counterpoint, and it came out in 1961 so the era is right on.

It wasn't all modernity. Bal a Versailles by Jean Despez (www.lessenteurs.com) is Barbarella-meets-Bond-Girl, sophisticated but with an ounce of depravation. It often evades description as the formula is incredibly dense and kalaedoscopic. Naughty brides should wear this, or the more contemporary L'Air de Rien by Miller Harris (www.millerharris.com). And, as a reminder that what goes around comes around, we have Balenciaga's Fleeting Moment; packed with soapy aldehydes, it has the feel of a tribute to Chanel No. 5. Want to sample an alternative? Try, um, Chanel No. 5.

1970S

The 70s is one of the most fun decades for fragrances, the huge diversity of scents belying the dreary economic situation on the streets. Anaïs Anaïs by Cacharel surely marks the pinnacle of the era. Sweet, gently sherbety flowers signaled white lace and demureness, though the wearer just might go out into the meadows for a proverbial roll in the hay. Penhaligon's Orange Blossom from its Anthology range of scents (www.penhaligons.com) is just as sunny, in which the orange blossom is joined by peach flower. A summer country wedding in a bottle.

If Cacharel is the demure little sister, then Diorella is the sassy big sister. Think Diane Keaton in an early Woody Allen film. If I had to buy a friend a bottle of perfume and knew nothing of her tastes, this is one I'd go for. It offers an amazing balancing act of elegance, swagger, and prettiness, with a mango-like mossiness to die for. It's still around, though sadly not in the original houndstooth bottle.

We can't really cover the 1970s without touching on the blockbuster genre: orientals. Opium may have ruled the roost, especially after its outrageously decadent launch party on a recreated opium barge. But the obsolete Mystere by Rochas was in the same vein, as was Dioressence, still on the shelves, with its spiciness taking patchouli out of the hippy domain and into an altogether richer territory. For a contemporary equivalent, Musc Ravageur by Frederic Malle (www.fredericmalle.com) is suitably balsamic and depraved, and reminds me of Coca-Cola in the best possible way.

The 70s had another beauty, which is rarely discussed: Nahema by Guerlain (www.guerlain.com). This is rose on steroids. If you'd gone to Studio 54 wearing this, you'd have toppled Bianca Jagger from her horse. You might topple the groom with this one. He'll need reviving.

PHOTOGRAPHY & FILM

As a wedding blogger, I see thousands of images every week, which vary in style and polish. This experience has come to teach me something very important about wedding photography. Aside from your wedding dress, on which you may want to lay out a small fortune (and who would blame you?), I cannot recommend highly enough that you focus a realistic portion of your wedding budget on securing the *very best* photographer that you can afford. Your wedding photographs will become treasured possessions— memories you can laugh and smile about in years to come with your family and a wonderful visual reminder of one of the most important days in your life. Be sensible, spend your money wisely, and try to avoid scrimping and saving—a good wedding photographer is worth her weight in gold.

Do your research on fees well in advance so that you can get a realistic idea of how much a good photographer, and all the services she will provide, costs. Fees will vary from photographer to photographer—and each photographer will offer a different kind of service, so it's important to do your homework and find out precisely what you will get for your money. Inquire if the photographer will have an assistant on the day to ensure all key photo opportunities aren't missed (e.g., will the photographer be able to cover *both* the bride's and groom's "getting ready" shots at the start of the day if you want them?). Check to see if the fees include albums and/or images on a disc. Confirm that the

photographer has experience, and is comfortable, with working at different times of the year—shooting in the depths of winter, for instance, when natural light is limited, can be a challenge. And ask if the photographer's services include a pre-wedding shoot—these really are super opportunities to learn to relax in front of the camera before your wedding day—perfect for the camera shy amongst us!

Almost all wedding photographers these days maintain a blog that is updated regularly with their most recent work (look for weddings that have been photographed *recently* as a sign that the photographer is in demand). Many also provide samples of their work via online portfolios—some even share their work via professional Facebook pages.

Visit your favorite wedding blogs (www.lovemydress.net is a great place to start) and if you love the way a particular wedding has been photographed, look up the photographer and make an inquiry. But do remember that good photographers will often get booked up many months in advance, so make sure you give yourself plenty of time to request their services.

Look out for crisp, clean photography with good, consistent quality and images that burst with wedding day happiness. Most importantly, look for images that make a real connection with you on a personal level. Each photographer has her own style—see how she approaches portrait and detail shots and consider her editing style. You want images that make you go "wow!"

I adore photography that is shot on traditional film (as opposed to digital capture), because of the beautiful color tones and soft, grainy quality of the imagery. Although most photographers shoot in digital, film photography has had a bit of a renaissance of late and there are some amazing film photographers to be found.

I find myself increasingly recommending putting money aside to have your wedding day documented as a film. This isn't something that everyone can afford, but I've come to view it as a beautiful and valuable investment for the future.

Above: Mark W. Brown (www.markwbrown.com) is a specialist in Super 8 mm film production, and travels the world recording films in this format. He describes retro-style film as "beautiful, timeless, and authentic" and comments that "a lot of couples are rediscovering this format and falling in love with it . . . how it brings back memories of their childhood, their parents and grandparents. They are almost reacquainting themselves with film like a long lost relative."

It is incredible how special memories can be evoked through watching film footage of your wedding day. For truly authentic "vintage" wedding film, look to a supplier who records using old home movie film, or Super 8 mm format. Super 8 mm is a film format that was widely used in the 1960s and 70s, before video reared its mighty head. Unlike video, that (nowadays) records the footage electronically onto a memory card, Super 8 prints the footage onto a roll of film, creating a wonderfully unique and timeless image.

LABELS TO LOOK FOR

Most vintage dresses dating between the Edwardian era and the 1940s will be label-free, but there are some designer labels you can look out for from the 50s, 60s, and 70s whose wedding dresses reflect the very greatest quality of production. The following list will guide you. The designer names have been placed into their strongest era, although many span three decades. Most of these designers would have created some bridalwear, but on the whole it is their evening gowns that are now sought after as wedding dresses.

1950S – 60S

John Cavanagh, Norman Hartnell, Sophie Gimbel, Madame Grès, Christian Dior, Pierre Balmain, Jacques Fath, Harvey Berin, Sybil Connoll, Ronald Paterson, and Jacques Heim are all outstanding couture names – their dresses are rare and very valuable. If you have the budget (!), there are still some out there – try www.thefrock.com.

For exciting, high-quality debutant, evening, and cocktail dresses with interesting provenance, look out particularly for some of the American designers and brands from the 50s and 60s. Many of these are being rediscovered at the moment. They often have strong notations of European couture, great cut and elaborate trims, reflecting the new era of American wealth and the post-war desire for escapist glamour. Look out for Lorrie Deb, Fred Perlberg, Lilli Diamond, Mr. Blackwell, and Harry Keiser.

Other important labels include Suzy Perette/Gigi Young, Hattie Carnegie, Will Steinman, and Edward Abbott. Some of these labels may have produced small bridal ranges, but even their white "coming out" gowns, or beautiful cream and white cocktail and eveningwear, are highly collectable for today's vintage-loving bride.

Specific bridalwear labels from the 50s, 60s, and even 70s include Emma Domb (also partywear) Sylvia Ann Bridal Originals, Priscilla of Boston, Bianchi, and William Cahill – all of whom are highly prized by specialized vintage wedding dress suppliers today. Vintage department store labels such as Saks Fifth Avenue and Harrods are also great finds for bridalwear.

1960S – 70S

Look out for Malcolm Starr, Gene Shelly (for elaborately beaded gowns), Mike Benet, Ossie Clark, Halston, Gunne Sax/Jessica McClintock, Laura Ashley, and Bill Gibb. On the whole, these designers were not bridalwear specific, but their designs make wonderful gowns for today's unique bride.

SUPPLIERS

An international selection – many ship worldwide.

ALEXANDRA KING
www.alexandra-king.com Vintage-inspired bespoke bridal and ready-to-wear cocktail dresses, handmade in the UK.

ANNIE'S VINTAGE CLOTHING
www.anniesvintageclothing.co.uk An amazing collection of quirky dresses – there's a constant supply of original 20s gowns with silk underslips.

BASIA ZARZYCKA
www.basia-zarzycka.com Romantic couture bridal gowns and vintage inspired accessories.

BELLE & BUNTY
www.belleandbunty.co.uk London-based duo Hannah and Alice offer an exquisitely designed vintage-inspired bridalwear collection.

BLUE BRIDALWEAR
www.bluebridalwear.co.uk Silk wedding gowns in classic silhouettes from the 50s and 60s. Perfect for an Audrey Hepburn-inspired bride.

CANDY ANTHONY
www.candyanthony.com Fun and colorful range of gowns, inspired by the 50s and 60s.

CAROLINE ATELIER BRIDALWEAR
www.caroline-atelier.com (available exclusively via Luella's Boudoir **www.luellasboudoir.co.uk**).

CHARLOTTE CASADÉJUS
http://charlottecasadejus.com Wedding gowns inspired by the style and elegance of the past.

CIRCA VINTAGE BRIDES
www.circabrides.com Astral Sundholm-Hayes's silk gowns exude the glamour of past decades.

CLAIRE PETTIBONE
www.clairepettibone.com Exquisite feminine clothing designed to combine a vintage feeling with modern style.

THE COUTURE COMPANY

www.the-couture-company.co.uk Custom-made beautiful, unusual, and unique bridalwear.

DANA BOLTON

www.dressmakingdesign.co.uk Bespoke gowns made from the finest silks and French lace. Dana's designs are romantic with a bohemian edge, reminiscent of the 30s and 40s.

DAUGHTERS OF SIMONE

http://daughtersofsimone.com Online vintage and vintage-inspired bridal store based in San Francisco. Many of the designs feature soft, bohemian details. Also available through www.etsy.com/shop/DaughtersOfSimone.

DEAR GOLDEN

www.etsy.com/shop/DearGolden An expertly curated online vintage store.

DISCOVER VINTAGE

www.discovervintage.co.uk Quality retailer of vintage clothes, shoes, handbags, jewelry and homeware from the 30s through the 70s.

DOLLY COUTURE

http://dollycouture.com Specialists in full-skirted, cocktail-length wedding gowns reminiscent of the 50s and early 60s.

DORIS DESIGNS

http://dorisdesigns.co.uk High quality petticoat skirts, also available in children's sizes.

ELIZABETH AVEY

www.elizabethavey.co.uk A dreamy collection of gorgeous, original vintage wedding dresses, dating from the 1900s to the 70s.

THE ENGLISH DEPT

www.etsy.com/shop/englishdept Romantic custom-made wedding dresses that echo styles and silhouettes of the past.

FAITH CATON-BARBER

www.faithbarber.com Bespoke bridalwear.

FLOSSY AND DOSSY

www.etsy.com/shop/flossyanddossy Independent dress designer specialising in "50s

glamour with a twist of twee." The range includes classic tea-length gowns and cute wiggle dresses, as well as some excellent options for bridesmaids.

THE FROCK

www.thefrock.com High-fashion original vintage dresses with an impressive collection of designer wedding gowns.

FUR COAT NO KNICKERS

www.furcoatnoknickers.co.uk Boutique where you can create the vintage wedding dress of your dreams using their vast collection of gowns that can be customized to size and taste.

GLORY DAYS VINTAGE

www.glorydaysvintage.co.uk Vintage original and bespoke replica wedding dresses from every decade of the 20th century.

THE GODDESS ROOM

www.thegoddessroom.net Original vintage wedding dresses and vintage Japanese kimonos.

HALFPENNY LONDON

www.halfpennylondon.com Fashion stylist and designer Kate Halfpenny is famed for her exquisite designs that take inspiration from bygone eras.

HEAVENLY VINTAGE BRIDES

www.heavenlyvintagebrides.co.uk Vintage gowns carefully sourced from around the world.

HEIRLOOM COUTURE

www.heirloomcouture.com Vintage-inspired made-to-measure and bespoke bridalwear.

HONEYPIE BOUTIQUE

http://honeypieboutique.co.uk Affordable 50s-inspired dresses and net petticoats.

HOPE & HARLEQUIN

www.hopeandharlequin.com Specializing in unique wedding dresses, they also offer bespoke vintage re-creations.

JACQUELINE BYRNE

www.jacquelinebyrne.co.uk Vintage-inspired bespoke wedding dresses featuring the finest silks, French lace, and intricate hand beading.

JENNY PACKHAM

www.jennypackham.com One of the UK's bestselling bridal designers, known for her elegant draping, Grecian-style gowns, and embellishment.

JOANNE FLEMING

www.joanneflemingdesign.com The studio offers bespoke gowns fashioned from silk, tulle, baroque-figured damask, and fine French lace in shapes with a clear vintage subtext.

KATHERINE FEIEL

www.katherinefeiel.com Bespoke and one-of-a-kind designer gowns, crafted from new and vintage fabrics. Canadian-based Feiel ships worldwide.

KATYA KATYA SHEHURINA

http://new.shehurina.com Feminine and playful wedding dresses from Latvian fashion designer Katya Shehurina. The collection includes beautiful vintage-inspired lace dresses that can be adjusted in length and color by mixing white dresses with colored slips, and 1920s-style drop-waist gowns.

LELUXE CLOTHING CO.

www.leluxeclothing.com Affordable beaded and tassled 1920s flapper-style gowns.

MINNA

www.minna.co.uk Eco-luxe bridal and evening-wear in whimsical, romantic silhouettes inspired by the styles of the 60s and 70s.

OH MY HONEY DRESSES

http://ohmyhoney.bigcartel.com/products Playful, handmade, 50s-inspired dresses.

OOH LA LA! VINTAGE

www.oohlalavintage.com An archive collection of French vintage fashion and accessories.

POSH GIRL VINTAGE

www.poshgirlvintage.com California-based collection of original vintage wedding dresses.

SALLY LACOCK

www.sallylacock.com Timeless vintage-inspired wedding dresses in antique tones. Dresses are adorned with hand-sewn silk flowers, distinctive glass buttons, and vintage details.

SASSI HOLFORD

www.sassiholford.com British designer Sassi references the past in many of her designs.

SASSO

www.sassobridalaccessories.net Boutique specializing in glamorous 30s-style marabou and ostrich-feather shrugs. They also carry a range of beautiful designer gloves and hats.

STATE OF GRACE

www.thestateofgrace.com London boutique offering bespoke garment and accessory design, personalized styling, and expert hair and make-up.

SUZANNAH

www.suzannah.com A nostalgic collection of bridalwear that perfectly combines vintage charm with modern vibrancy. Suzannah's famous 30s-inspired tea dresses are particularly special.

UNFORGETTABLE VINTAGE BRIDAL GOWNS

www.vintagebridalgowns.co.uk A delicious collection of original vintage wedding and bridesmaid dresses.

VICKY ROWE

www.vickyrowe.co.uk A selection of 1920s and flapper-inspired beaded wedding dresses.

THE VINTAGE BRIDE

www.thevintagebride.com Online boutique with dresses ranging from pre-WWII to the 1960s.

VINTAGE FUR HIRE

www.vintage-fur-hire.co.uk Re-crafted and recycled vintage furs available for hire.

THE VINTAGE WEDDING DRESS COMPANY

www.vwdc.co.uk Showroom with unique range of original vintage wedding dresses, complemented by a capsule collection of vintage-inspired gowns.

VIVIEN OF HOLLOWAY

www.vivienofholloway.com Specialize in replica 1950s clothing, with a fabulous line of bridalwear and a variety of dresses perfect for bridesmaids.

WHIRLING TURBAN

http://whirlingturban.com Vintage reproduction bridalwear and pin-up couture in quality fabrics.

ZOE LEM

http://zoelem.co.uk A collection of wedding dresses celebrating classic vintage styles from the 20s to the 60s, along with the ideal body shapes for each era.

ACCESSORIES

ANN GUISE SILK WEDDING VEILS

http://crowningglorysilkveils.homestead.com Silk tulle wedding veils professionally designed and handmade to order using only high quality silk, lace, and embroidery.

BABA-C

www.baba-c.co.uk Unique and handcrafted vintage-inspired tiaras, veils, capes, jewelry, and bridal accessories.

BETH MORGAN

www.bethmorgan.co.uk A couture milliner offering a fabulous range of bridal fascinators.

BRITTEN

www.brittenweddings.co.uk Handmade feather fans, deco-inspired purses, statement headbands, hair combs, garters, and bouttonnieres.

CHERISHED

www.cherishedvintage.co.uk Eclectic collection of delicate tiaras, headbands and hairpins fashioned from vintage treasures. They can also create bespoke pieces using your own jewelry.

CORNELIA JAMES

www.corneliajames.com Glove manufacturers with a broad collection of elegant bridal gloves.

CRYSTAL DELICA

www.crystaldelica.com Bespoke range of bridal accessories that successfully marry the old with the new to create unique, breathtaking pieces.

DEBBIE CARLISLE BOUQUETS

www.dcbouquets.co.uk One-off vintage brooch and button bouquets and bridal headpieces.

DONNA CRAIN

www.donnacrain.com Specializes in creating eclectic headpieces and veils.

FLO & PERCY

www.floandpercy.com Hair accessories and tiaras.

HF COUTURE

www.hfcouture.co.uk Bridal accessories and headpieces inspired by the romance of yesteryear.

THE HOUSE OF KAT SWANK

www.etsy.com/shop/thehouseofkatswank Range of handmade theatrical fascinators, headpieces, and other textile art accessories crafted with vintage elements.

HOUSE OF ISTRIA

www.houseofistria.com A range of handcrafted hair accessories.

HT HEADWEAR

www.htheadwear.com Gorgeous range of millinery finished with an array of vintage details.

JANE TAYLOR MILLINERY

www.janetaylormillinery.com Distinctive vintage-inspired millinery.

JO BARNES

www.jobarnesvintage.com Luxury range of award-winning accessories handcrafted from vintage jewelry, Swarovski crystals, and pearls.

LILA

www.lila-lila.com Greek-born designer Lila crafts the most beautiful clay headband and floral crown headpieces. This up and coming designer has a beautiful unique signature style.

LISA HARRIS JEWELLERY

www.lisaharrisjewellery.co.uk Exquisite vintage-inspired headpieces and jewelry.

LOVE BY SUSIE

www.lovebysusie.co.uk Veils, Juliet caps, and wedding lingerie.

LUCY MARSHALL

www.lucymarshall.com Beautiful 20s- and 30s-style headpieces and delicate bridal gloves.

MADELINE BRIDE

www.madeleinebride.com Beautiful handcrafted bridal veils and headpieces.

MUSCARI WHITES
www.muscariwhites.co.uk Creators of bespoke, jeweled, vintage bridal bouquets.

PASSIONATE ABOUT VINTAGE
http://passionateaboutvintage.co.uk Specialist in vintage wedding jewelry.

PEARLS AND SWINE
www.pearlsandswine.bigcartel.com Vintage-Inspired millinery, bespoke headwear and avant-garde fascinators.

PINKHAM MILLINERY
www.pinkhammillinery.com Handmade hats created by Dayna Pinkham in Portland, Oregon.

POSH VEILS
www.poshveils.com Canadian-based Sharon Chironda designs veils inspired by the past.

RENE WALRUS
www.renewalrus.co.uk Vintage-inspired tiaras, fascinators, and bridal jewelry.

ROSIE WEIZENCRANTZ
www.rosieweisencrantz.com Whimsical, mystical, vintage-inspired statement jewelry.

SHARPER MILLINERY
www.sharpermillinery.co.uk Hat and headpiece designer who takes inspiration from all eras.

SHEENA HOLLAND
www.sheenaholland.com Vintage-style feather headbands and wedding headpieces.

SILVER SIXPENCE IN HER SHOE
www.silver-sixpence-in-her-shoe.co.uk Bespoke vintage-inspired bridal accessories.

STRUMPET BRIDE
www.etsy.com/shop/strumpetbride Retro-style bridal cocktail hats with a twist on 50s/60s chic.

TWIGS AND HONEY
www.twigsandhoney.com Exquisite headpieces, veils, bridal caps, belts, and tiaras.

VICTORIA MILLÉSIME
www.victoriamillesime.co.uk Timeless bridal caps, statement headpieces, sashes, and jewelry.

VINTAGE BRIDAL JEWELLERY
www.vintagebridaljewellery.co.uk Vintage jewelry, headpieces, and handbags.

VINTAGE MAGPIE
www.vintagemagpie.co.uk Exquisite, sparkling jeweled bouquets with original vintage elements.

VIVIEN SHERIFF
www.viviensheriff.co.uk Beautifully produced bridal headpieces and veils.

SHOES
EMMY
www.emmyshoes.co.uk London-based bespoke shoe maker specializing in vintage-inspired heels.

FREYA ROSE
http://freyarose.com Freya's bridal collection incorporates freshwater pearls, couture Parisian lace, and heels adorned in mother-of-pearl.

HARRIET WILDE
www.harrietwilde.com Unique bridal footwear, including fabulous 70s-style platform heels.

HETTY ROSE
www.hettyrose.co.uk Shoes crafted by reworking vintage materials.

RACHEL SIMPSON
www.rachelsimpsonshoes.co.uk Vintage-inspired bridal shoes, shipping worldwide.

PROPS AND STYLING
CHERRYTIME
www.etsy.com/shop/cherrytIme A delightful selection of knitted, crocheted, and hand-felted wedding cake toppers and boutonnieres.

HALO AND MEME
www.etsy.com/shop/HaloandMeme Unique wedding centerpieces created from vintage books.

LILLE SYSTER
www.etsy.com/shop/lillesyster Handmade paper flower garlands, loose paper flowers, and wedding décor.

LITTLE RETREATS
www.etsy.com/shop/LittleRetreats Cool handmade photobooth props and signs.

PAPER POM-POMS
www.paperpoms.co.uk Pretty paper pom-poms of all shapes, sizes, and shades..

TWO SISTERS
www.etsy.com/shop/TwoSistersOldAndNew A fabulous store for sourcing vintage handkerchiefs for use as wedding invitations and favors, or simply to gift to your bridesmaids.

THE VINTAGE DRAWER
www.etsy.com/shop/vickytrainor Beautiful handmade wedding stationery and décor crafted from reclaimed vintage linens and notions.

ENTERTAINMENT
A-TOWN BOOKING AGENCY AND EVENTS
http://www.oldtimey.net Providing exclusive representation for a host of West Coast-based artists who play jump, western swing, rhythm & blues, blues, and rockabilly, including Stompy Jones, West Coast Ramblers, The B-Stars, and DJ Tanoa "Samoa Boy," they're sure to provide the vintage hits to suit your day.

AUSTIN PHONOGRAPH COMPANY
http://austinphonographcompany.com/ Specializing in music from the 1930s, the Austin Phonograph Company provides hand-cranked entertainment.

THE FAT BABIES
http://thefatbabies.com/ This exciting seven-piece jazz band from Chicago beautifully interprets classic styles of the 1920s and 30s.

THE FLAT CATS
www.flatcatsmusic.com The Flat Cats play a range of the hottest swinging jazz and blues, contemporary classics, and timeless standards. They're able to tailor their style and sound to fit your special event.

MICHAEL CUMELLA'S CRANK-UP PHONOGRAPH DJ EXPERIENCE

http://michaelcumella.com/phonographdj/index.html Cumella has been the host of WFMU's Antique Phonograph Music Program since 1995 and is an expert on music from 1900 to 1929.

ROYAL SOCIETY JAZZ ORCHESTRA

http://rsjo.com/ Renowned for performing big band swing, 1920s jazz, blues, Dixieland, as well as vintage and traditional jazz in and around San Francisco.

THE SONS OF SUSAN

http://www.sonsofsusan.com Based in Chicago, the Sons of Susan play jazz, blues, swing, and western swing.

THE VINTAGE DJ

http://www.vintagedj.com With an eclectic mix of records from the 30s, 40s, 50s, 60s, and Early 70s, he can take your guests to a Prohibition Era speakeasy, a roadside juke-joint, a mod London hotspot, or an explosive Afro-Cuban nightclub.

STATIONERY

ARTCADIA

www.artcadia.co.uk Beautiful, original digital and letterpress wedding stationery.

BERINMADE

www.berinmade.com Colorful, quirky, retro-inspired stationery by designer Erin Hung.

CUTTURE

www.cutture.com Specialists in laser-cut stationery that can be tailored to requirements.

EMILY & JO

www.emilyandjo.co.uk Classic couture stationery.

GOGOSNAP VINTAGE CORRESPONDENCE

www.etsy.com/shop/GoGoSnap Invitations created from a personal collection of original vintage art and photography.

HELLO LUCKY!

www.hellolucky.co.uk Specialist letterpress printer and design studio with offices in San Francisco and London.

I AM NAT

www.iamnat.co.uk Retro/vintage-inspired wedding and occasion stationery.

IN THE TREEHOUSE

www.inthetreehouse.co.uk Lovely personalized wedding stationery with lots of vintage and retro design options.

LETTERBOX INK

www.etsy.com/shop/LetterBoxInk Custom wedding invitations influenced by vintage travel, tickets, and ephemera.

RSVP CANDY

www.rsvpcandy.com Unique, personalized retro wedding invitations.

SUGALILY

www.sugalily.co.uk Quirky, retro-inspired design.

BLOGS AND ONLINE READING

GREEN WEDDING SHOES

http://greenweddingshoes.com Showcases the most inspirational weddings in the US and beyond.

LONDON BRIDE

http://london-bride.com Stylist Charley Beard's wedding blog regularly features vintage and retro-inspired weddings styled by Charley herself.

LOVE MY DRESS

www.lovemydress.net The UK's leading vintage-inspired wedding blog.

A NATURAL WEDDING

www.thenaturalweddingcompany.co.uk Online directory and blog for eco-friendly, seasonal, vintage, and handmade weddings.

RUFFLED BLOG

http://ruffledblog.com Blog offering beautiful vintage-inspired weddings and handmade DIY wedding ideas.

SNIPPET AND INK

www.snippetandink.com Curates unique and meaningful wedding day inspiration that regularly features retro and vintage-inspired weddings.

STYLE ME PRETTY

www.stylemepretty.com Major wedding blog featuring a daily selection of inspirational real weddings, DIY, and styling ideas.

WEDDING CHICKS

www.weddingchicks.com Wedding blog which features many vintage and retro inspired real weddings.

WHIMSICAL WONDERLAND WEDDINGS

http://whimsicalwonderlandweddings.com A UK wedding blog offering an eclectic mix of inspirational weddings.

FILMMAKERS

BAYLY & MOORE

www.baylymoore.com US-based producers who use stop motion to create quirky, alternative, and beautifully crafted wedding films.

MARK BROWN

www.markwbrown.com One of the best Super 8mm film producers in the UK, who travels worldwide to take on wedding film commissions.

MINTYSLIPPERS

www.mintyslippers.com A UK-based bespoke film company with a passion for telling stories via film. Mintyslippers regularly travel around the world to film their clients.

REELLOVE FILMS

www.reellovefilms.co.uk Gorgeous, bespoke, and natural wedding film and video, offering full international coverage.

ACKNOWLEDGMENTS

This book is dedicated to my loving and supportive husband Philip and two little girls, Eska Eleanor and Leanora Rose, whose unconditional love amazes and inspires me every day, and who were so patient with Mummy while she "disappeared" for several months to focus on writing this book.

I would also like to dedicate this book to my darling grandma Edna who sadly passed away in 2011. Researching the book transported me back to the time my grandma tied the knot in the 1940s. This experience made me appreciate more than ever how lucky we are to live during times when, for many of us, weddings can be celebrated just how we want, and not in an environment blighted by war. Grandma, you made such a beautiful bride, and I am so proud to be able to dedicate this book in your honor.

Becoming a published author for the very first time is a dream come true, and I am bursting with pride and joy. But by no means am I solely responsible for this accomplishment — I am exceptionally privileged to work alongside many brilliant people in the wedding industry, whose hard work, creativity, support, and advice has been vital to the production of this book. I am so lucky to call many of these people my friends, as well as colleagues, and it is important to me that I say thanks here.

First and foremost, I need to thank my readers, sponsors, and all those who support my blog, Love My Dress (www.lovemydress.net). Through Love My Dress, I have been introduced to many like-minded souls who have inspired me in ways I never thought possible: brides (and grooms!), photographers, filmmakers, designers, creators, curators, purveyors of pretty things. My world has changed almost beyond recognition since launching Love My Dress and I am so proud watching the blog go from strength-to-strength as I work with an expanding team of writers and contributors to extend its appeal. All these people, who contribute towards making Love My Dress so successful, are the reason my name is on the front of this book — thank you from the bottom of my heart for all your support.

The biggest thank you EVER to the photoshoot team.

Photographer Joanna Brown (www.joannabrownphotography.com)

Stylist, vintage shape expert, and advisor Zoe Lem (www.zoelem.co.uk)

Hair Severin Hubert of Hepburn Collection (www.hepburncollection.com)

Make-up Amanda Moorhouse of Lipstick & Curls (www.lipstickandcurls.net)

Vintage manicure specialist Sharon of Minnie Moons (www.facebook.com/pages/Minnie-Moons/172819142802587)

Stylist (décor) Michelle Kelly of Pocketful of Dreams (www.pocketfulofdreams.co.uk)

Props advisor Kate Fletcher of Vintage Style Hire (www.vintagestylehire.co.uk)

Scent specialist Lizze Ostrum, aka Odette Toilette (www.scratchandsniffevents.com)

Models The beautiful Claire, Sarah C, Ivana, Tahuonia, Gia, and Rebecca, thanks to Zone Models (www.zone models.com)

Film Production Frances of Reellove Films

Photoshoot assistants My darling husband; Leyla Seydo; Lizzie Jones (www.weddingyurts.co.uk)

Thanks to the many amazing suppliers who so willingly agreed to donate their time, expertise, and beautiful products and services to the photoshoot: **Artcadla, Berinmade, Beautiful Bird Creations, Belle and Bunty, Tyler Branch, Blush Floral Design, Charlotte Casadéjus, Eliza Claire, Emma Case, The Couture Company, Candy Anthony, Cherished Vintage, Christopher Currie Photography, Circa Vintage Brides, The Cotton Candy Girls, Cutture, Dana Bolton, Lisa Devlin, Doris Designs, Dottie Creations, Edwina Ibbotson, Elizabeth Avey, Emily & Jo, Emmy Shoes, Debs Ivelja, Freya Rose, Fur Coat No Knickers, Steve Gerrard, Harriet Wilde Shoes, Heavenly Vintage Brides, Hetty Rose Shoes, Sheena Holland, House of Istria, HT Headwear, Jo Barnes Vintage, Joanne Fleming, Katya Katya Shehurina, Lila, Lucy Marshall, Luella's Boudoir, Anneli Marinovich, James Melia, Graham Morgan, Olofson Design, Madeline Bride, McKinley Rodgers, Paper Poms, Rosie Parsons, Ed Peers, Poppy Children, The Real Cut Flower Garden, Vicky Rowe, Sally Lacock, Shoot Lifestyle Photography, Rachel Simpson Shoes, Britt J. Spring, The State of Grace, Studio 1208, Nick Tucker, Unforgettable Vintage Brides, The Utterly Sexy Cafe, Victoria Millésime, Vicky Trainor, Vintage Fur Hire, Vowed and Amazed, and Zoe Clark Cakes.**

Thanks also to our photoshoot venue Dalston Heights (www.dalstonheights.com) and to the Hoxton Hotel for so kindly providing storage and accommodation.

A special mention to Emma Woodhouse, aka The Wedding Reporter (http://theweddingreporter.co.uk), for being such a brilliant supporter of Love My Dress, to Laura Caudery of Parallel Venues (http://parallelvenues.co.uk) for her invaluable advice, wisdom, friendship, and support, and finally to the absolutely wonderful Franky (www.love-audrey.com) — the best teammate anyone could wish for. I could not have done this without Franky's support and encouragement. Love you lots Franks xx.

I must give special thanks to my lovely Mum and Dad and my parents-in-law for all their support and encouragement.

Thanks also to Naomi Thompson (www.naomithompson.co.uk) for her recommendation to Anova Books.

Finally, huge thanks to my commissioning editor Emily Preece-Morrison and her team at Anova Books, and to my publishing agent Rebecca Winfield.

Annabel xXx

This edition published in the USA in 2013 by Chicago Review Press, Incorporated.

First published in the United Kingdom by Pavilion Books, an imprint of Anova Books Company Ltd.

First published in the United Kingdom in 2013 by PAVILION BOOKS an imprint of Anova Books Company Ltd.
10 Southcombe Street, London, UK W14 0RA

"Style Me Vintage" is a registered trademark of Anova Books Ltd.

Text © Annabel Beeforth, 2013
Design and layout © Anova Books, 2013
Photography © Anova Books, except those listed in Picture Credits

Chicago Review Press Incorporated
814 North Franklin Street
Chicago, Illinois 60610
ISBN 978-1-61374-811-4

Colour reproduction by Rival Colour Ltd., UK
Printed and bound by Toppan Leefung Printing Ltd., China

PICTURE CREDITS

All special photography by Joanna Brown except those credited below.
©: p.5: Karen McGowran (www.karenmcgowran.co.uk); pp.12-13, 16-17: Shoot Lifestyle Photography (www.shoot-lifestyle.co.uk); p.14T and B: from the collection of Annabel Beeforth; p.15L: Vintage Image/Alamy; p.15R: Corbis; pp.18-19: Anneli Marinovich (www.annelimarinovich.com); p.22L: Condé Nast Archive/Corbis; p.22R: Mary Evans/Vanessa Wagstaff Collection; p.23T: collection of Annabel Beeforth; p.23B: Illustrated London News Ltd/Mary Evans; p.23R: Mary Evans/Jazz Age Club Collection; p.38: Debs Ivelja (www.debsijelva.com); pp.40-41: Rosie Parsons(www.rosieparsons.com); p.44L: from the collection of Kirsten Mavric (www.kirstenmavric.co.uk); p.44R: Mary Evans/Vanessa Wagstaff Collection; p.45L: Mary Evans/National Magazines; p.45TR: from the collection of Annabel Beeforth; p.45BR: Condé Nast Archive/Corbis; p.60L: James Melia (www.jamesmelia.com); pp.62-63: Ed Peers (www.edpeers.com); pp.64-65: Lisa Devlin (http://devlinphotos.co.uk); p.68L: ClassicStock/Corbis; p.68R: Minnesota Historical Society/Corbis; p.69TL: from the collection of Chelsea of Pastel Pirate (http://theweddingfestival.blogspot.com); p.69B: from the collection of Annabel Beeforth; p.69R: Illustrated London News Ltd/Mary Evans; p.83L and R: Becky Mitchell (www.beckymitchell.co.uk); pp84-87: Eliza Claire (http://elizaclaire.com); p.90L: Mary Evans Picture Library/National Magazine Company; p.90R: Illustrated London News Ltd/Mary Evans; p.91L: from the collection of Eve Phillips; p.91TR: Mary Evans Picture Library; p.91BR: from the collection of Annabel Beeforth; p.94L: Robert Lawler (www.robertlawler.co.uk); p.109: Steve Gerrard (www.stevegerrardphotography.com); pp.110-111: McKinley Rodgers Photography (http://mckinley-rodgers.com/blog); pp.112-113: Nick Tucker Photography (www.blog.nicktuckerphotography.com); p.116L: from the collection of Yemi Kosibah (www.kosibah.co.uk); p.116R: Bettmann/Corbis; p.117L: V&A Images/Alamy; p.117TR: from the collection of Polly Alexandre; p.117BR: from the collection of Annabel Beeforth; p.118: James Melia; p.120L and R: Cotton Candy Weddings (www.cottoncandyweddings.co.uk); pp.134-135: Christopher Currie Photography (www.christophercurrie.co.uk); pp.136-137: Graham Morgan (www.grahammorgan.com); p.140L and R: Mary Evans/Peter Akehurst; p.141TL: J. Wilds/Keystone/Getty Images; p.141B: Keystone/Getty Images; p.141R: from the collection of Alice Shreeve (www.belleandbunty.co.uk); pp.158-159: Tyler Branch Photography (http://tylerbranchphoto.com); p.168: Dasha Caffrey (www.dashacaffrey.com); p.169: Leila Scarfiotti.